Western Slope

Sharp End
publishing

by Phillip Benningfield

Mountain Biking Colorado's Western Slope

by Phillip Benningfield

copyright 2000 by Sharp End Publishing, LLC.

All rights reserved. This book or any part thereof may not be reproduced in any form without written permission from the publisher.

ISBN # 1-892540-11-8

Library of Congress Control Number 00-131518

For a complete list of titles available from Sharp End Publishing, please write to PO Box 1613, Boulder, CO 80306 or check us out on the web at www.sharpendbooks.com.

Sharp End Publishing is always looking for new material. Please send queries to the address above or email to inforock@aol.com.

Cover photo and content photos by Tom Zuccareno.
Photo of Dwayne Weedle, on pages 1 and 98 by Fred Knapp.

All Topographic maps and elevation profiles were created using Topo! To learn more about their products visit www.topo.com.

WARNING - Read this first

Mountain biking is by its very nature potentially hazardous. It is not within the scope of this book to disclose all the potential dangers. Good judgement and skill can help reduce the inherent risk.

THE PUBLISHER AND AUTHOR EXPRESSLY DISCLAIM ALL REPRESENTATIONS AND WARRANTIES REGARDING THIS GUIDE, THE ACCURACY OF THE INFORMATION CONTAINED HEREIN, AND THE RESULTS OF YOUR USE HEREOF, INCLUDING WITHOUT LIMITATION, IMPLIED WARRANTIES OF MERCHANTABILITY AND FITNESS FOR A PARTICULAR PURPOSE. THE USER ASSUMES ALL RISK ASSOCIATED WITH THIS GUIDE.

Be careful out there.

Table of Contents

Table of Contents

Introduction

If you love mountain biking and have not ventured to Colorado's Western Slope, quit your job, rob a bank, pack your car, load your bike, and get there. Fast. The biking terrain throughout this region of Colorado is as diverse as a New York City block and as superb as Led Zeppelin II. Trailheads begin throughout the mountains of the Roaring Fork Valley from Glenwood Springs to Aspen then travel west into the desert slickrock and canyons near Grand Junction and Fruita.

The thirty one trails selected for this guide are some of the very best. Inevitably someone's favorite trail will be omitted; however, it is likely that a great trail with similar attributes is in the guide. Access issues were a factor in trail choice as well. Many rides are not included because I felt they did not offer enjoyable riding or were in an area with far more popular trails.

Trails in this guide were picked based on three main criteria:
>   *Singletrack—Trails with a large amount of singletrack
>   received top priority in selection.
>   *Diversity—Trails with different environment, length,
>   commitment, climate and scenery were selected in order to
>   give the rider a wider range of choice.
>   *Flat Tops Wilderness—These adventurous trails are given
>   top billing—all are fresh for bikers.

Due to the great diversity of included rides, it is even more important that you pick your trails wisely. Some rides are on mini-mountain bike highways, while others, such as the Flat Tops trails, offer a serious feeling of adventure. Take times and distances with a huge handful of salt. You may find that a projected ride of two to four hours may require over six if you make a wrong turn.

Always be willing to come back to a trail another day rather than endure a drawn out epic in the cold and rain and dark. I only had an epic one time—well actually three times, while trying to discover a link on some ride that never made it into the guide anyway. The experience was, nonetheless, invigorating. Of course the hailstorm, downpour and ten-mile ride back to the car taught me a good lesson—bikers aren't immune to Colorado weather or hypothermia. Be wise and use common sense (your own or a friend's if necessary).

There you have my philosophy on the rides included in this guide. A few last tips are to stop and smell and flowers, think about the burgers and beer you will have when it's all over, and especially, take in the panoramic views on the sweet trails.

Acknowledgments:

I'll make it short and sweet. Writing a guidebook and collecting the information is not a one-person job. It is a humanitarian endeavor in which many people participate. There are so many people who helped: friends who built trails and put up with my never-ending capacity to screw up, waitresses who didn't sneer when I ordered two meals, bike mechanics who were true and helpful, and cashiers at beer stores. To all these people, whether or not you realized you were helping and making the pain go away, I thank you.

Tom Zuccareno and Z Photography
Eric Candee, trail-building guru and swale guy
Mindy Candee massage therapist master
Pat Deciccio and the Boulder Map Gallery
The Waugh clan
New York Pizza in Aspen
The mechanics at Over the Edge Sports in Fruita
University Bike Shop in Boulder
Cutting Edge Sports in Boulder
BSR Sports in Glenwood Springs
Dwayne Weedle and Spencer Hoffman in Grand Junction (thanks for the tour)

How to Use this Guide

Read all the Introductory pages first. There are many helpful tips to understand the icons, biking necessities and ride descriptions. It will save you from large blood clots when you get angry because the guide's clarity seems questionable.

1. Take a look at the **Trails Chart** (in the Appendix) to find what ride suits your tastes.

2. Go to the ride and look at **Time and Distance** then consider the Technical Difficulty last. Rides are given an overall rating, as well as an explanation on the technical level encountered. Generally, a ride with an Expert classification on difficulty only means you may have to walk the bike instead of ride for short distances.

3. Look at **Elevation**. The higher rides will be wet and impassable in early spring. It is also important to get in shape on lower rides before jumping up to a ride at 10,000 feet (unless you are crazy).

4. Look closely at the **Topographic Maps** and know how to read them properly. The map will be useless unless you have some orienteering skills.

5. Read the **Ride Description** and find creeks, drainages and canyons on the topographic map. Having a clue where landmarks are will make the obscure rides much smoother.

6. If a ride is in The Flat Tops, or at high elevation, bring **extra clothes, tools and water**. A compass might also be a good idea.

7. Pack the **guide** and go riding. Do not rely on memory. A thirty mile ride has far too many directions to retain from one measly reading.

8. Additional rides on Four Mile Park, and 2150 Trail are all brand new trails. Ride them at your own risk—you'd be a fool not to **bring a map** for these rides.

Ride Information

Each ride has an introductory description of the trail and
area. The descriptions highlight major landmarks (fences,
drainages and trail signs) as well as any transition from
singletrack to dirt road to pavement. Many of the rides will
be extremely obscure with a multitude of side trails that
lead off into no-man's land. If you find yourself questioning
a turn or trail, backtrack on the bike or in the book's
description to get the proper bearings. The only rides with
truly difficult trail-finding are in the Flat Tops, at Rifle and
a couple in the Roaring Fork Valley. And remember that
most of the rides are loops so a mountain or other major
landmark can always guide you home.

Directions: Most directions are given from Interstate 70
then leading off to the north or south to the beginning of
the ride. A few of the rides assume familiarity with the
vicinity of the ride and therefore give minor directions from
Carbondale, Aspen, etc.

Easy   **Advanced**   **Expert**

Ride Difficulty: Take this with a large container of salt.
Every rider has a different idea of what **Easy, Advanced**
and **Expert** means. In this book, rides are given an overall
rating that is denoted by the above symbols. The rating
generally comes from the technical requirements of the
ride. Physical difficulty can be found in both the description as well as looking at the elevation gain and mileage for
the ride.

Easy does not mean bike path; a certain level of skill is
needed just to ride off road. You may sometimes find
Expert sections within a ride designated **Advanced**. Don't
let this discourage you as usually only one difficult obstacle
must be dealt with. A less experienced rider can do all
Expert rides, but may be hiking with the bike for short
sections. In other words, do not be turned off on a ride by
its technical difficulty if the mileage and elevation total are
to your liking.

Time: Again, take this with a massive amount of salt. The shortest amount of time given on the rides is if the ride is done clean from start to finish. The greater time is for an out-of-shape couch potato that got a new bike for Christmas. Even the greatest time may not be conservative enough if you have not ridden singletrack for a decade or two.

Distance: You will come in a little under and over with all the little side trails you check out or find yourself lost on. The mileage in the ride descriptions is always rounded down (sometimes as much as a couple of tenths of a mile!)

Elevation Gain/Loss Total: This is an approximate assessment of the entire ups and downs on the rides based from the topographic maps. With the hundreds of small hills and creek crossings the totals are educated guesses at best.

Maps: The maps used in the guide have the same contour interval. All maps are oriented so that they read North up. Additional maps are given for further study—and absolutely suggested to use on less-traveled trails.

Observations: These tell you of things like: warnings of hunting season, the mountains you will see, and the best time of year for foliage.

Topo Legend

Indicates unsurfaced road or trail

Indicates improved dirt road or paved road

Biking Season

The best aspect of the rides is that there never needs to be a day all year where a trail cannot be ridden. Fruita and Grand Junction trails can be enjoyed in the depths of winter. In the blazing hot Colorado summer you can beat the heat by riding up in the Flat Tops or in the upper Roaring Fork or Crystal River Valleys.

What you need: The Neccessities

A tuned and functioning bike will help you avoid breakdowns, poor shifting, and hours of frustration filled with angry lamentations.

A tuned bike will have:
1. True wheels.
2. Chain, hubs and cables all lubed.
3. Properly shifting gears and bomber brakes.
4. Tight bolts on the headtube and cranks.
5. Wheels attached properly and not rubbing the brake pads.

Gear:
1. Clothes fitting the ride ahead: a waterproof shell or sleeves for legs and arms, full-finger gloves, a hat and warm vest are absolutely necessary in the mountains. A light shell is good at lower elevations.
2. A helmet. Always wear something to protect your skull!
3. Gloves to protect your hands from hours of bone-crushing terrain and inevitable wrecks.
4. Sunglasses.
5. A Camelback or other water/backpack combo is far better than water bottles and mounds of gear stuffed in a jersey.

Tools:
1. Tubes
2. Allen wrenches
3. Chain tool
4. Tire iron
5. Spoke tool
6. Tire patch kit
7. Chain lube
8. A multi-tool with screwdriver, wrenches and Allen wrenches.
9. Extra parts that can break: chain links, derailleur parts, cleats, Allen bolts, etc.

Nutrition:
1. Water. Do not underestimate how much water you will need. More than enough is perfect.
2. Take energy bars, bagels, fruit, or a nice turkey and provolone sandwich on the ride.
3. Asprin and Ibuprofen for long rides is very helpful when your lower back turns to a lump of pain.

Considerations

1. Closed Trails: If a trail has a seasonal closure, respect it! The worst thing a selfish biker can do is spoil every other biker's fun by getting a trail closed for good.

2. Hunting season: Best to avoid rides that will take you anywhere near the tired and trigger-happy men from Illinois and Iowa, trouncing through the woods with their guns. If you do a ride in hunters' paradise wear bright clothes, make a lot of noise and try to stay on well-traveled trails.

3. Weather: The skies can change in a matter of minutes. Lightning above treeline is truly dangerous, and being near it is truly terrifying. Hail hurts when you are riding to escape its bombardment; rain at 9000' is bitter cold; snow is frozen rain—need I say more. Always take into consideration the weather forecast, the skies and the elevation you are riding. A rainstorm in the desert is refreshing but can cause hypothermia at higher elevations.

4. Your physical condition: The first ride of the season after being a couch potato all winter should not be the longest ride in the guide. Do some of the short rides at lower elevation to get in shape. If you ride all year long then feel free to beat yourself up on the thirty-mile jaunts first.

IMBA Rules of the Trail

The International Mountain Biking Association has outlined standard trail behavior for mountain bikers. Access is fragile and many trails can be closed due to the rude and inconsiderate actions of a few. Do your part to keep trails open by following these rules.

1. Ride on open trails only.
Don't push access issues by trespassing on private land. It is not permitted to ride in federal and state wilderness.

2. Leave no trace.
Think low impact. Stay on existing trails and avoid riding when the soil condition is sensitive to erosion (after rain).

3. Control of your bike.
Pay attention to speed regulations, be alert in all situations.

4. Bikes must yield.
Make others aware of your presence by slowing down and speaking or gesturing in a friendly manner.

5. Never spook animals.
Animals can spook causing a dangerous situation if you race in front of them or come up quickly behind them. Leave gates as you encountered them.

6. Plan ahead.
Keep your equipment working, know where you are going, and plan for inclement weather. Don't forget your helmet!

Aspen

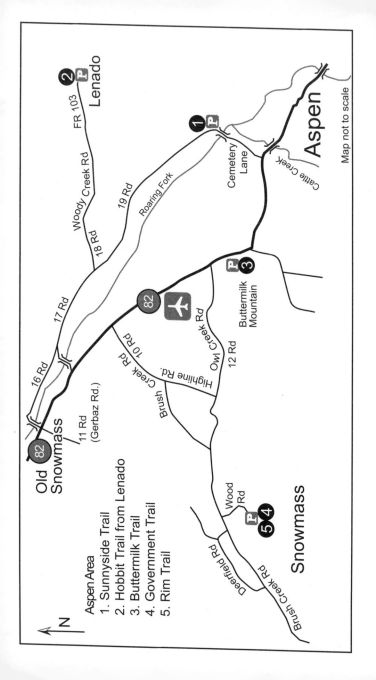

Sunnyside Trail

The Sunnyside is an exceptional ride in the upper Roaring Fork Valley. This ride offers panoramic views of Aspen, Highlands Mountain, the Maroon Bells and many other peaks. Expect to climb with gusto up long switchbacked dirt roads with the perfect reward of Sunnyside's harrowing singletrack descents. The climb on Sunnyside is for all levels but the descent will rattle the bones and will require a little walking for the faint of heart.

From Aspen take Cemetery Lane (just past the stoplight headed up to Aspen Highlands as one enters Aspen). Pass the cemetery on the right. Continue downhill, headed down valley, and cross the Roaring Fork River. Drive up a hill 0.6 mile and park in the parking lot on the left. This is next to Gold Butte and opposite the end of the Sunnyside Trail (a trail map is present).

Expert. Fast singletrack descents with rock obstacles, switchbacks and babyheads. Substantial hill climbs.

1.5 hours to 4 hours

15.3 miles

4220'

Pitkin County #2, Aspen, Thimble Rock

As with most rides at elevation the trail will be muddy and wet through the spring with numerous downed trees. This trail dries faster than the nearby Hobbit. Good brakes are absolutely necessary. Watch for hikers and other cyclists on this popular trail.

Sunnyside Trail mileage descriptions

0.0 Parking lot opposite the end of Sunnyside Trail descent. Head back down Cemetery Lane to Rio Grande Trail (paved bike path). Go left and skirt the Roaring Fork River.

0.3 Take left on Rio Grande Trail. Head upriver into Aspen.

2.1 Continue across intersected trail onto a gravel trail.

2.2 Next to Aspen Velo. Go left on North Mill Street.

2.3 Right on Gibson Avenue. Up a hill. Continue through two stop signs past a mobile home park. The road turns into Park Circle. Then go left on Silver Lode. Immediate right on Smuggler Mountain Road (dirt road). Steep and continuous through multiple switchbacks.

4.4 Overlook on right and views of construction. Road heads east from the overlook. The road splits. Take the left road. Do not go past a private road (straight). Views of Garret's, Daly, Snowmass and Highlands Bowl.

4.9 Barbed-wire fence on sides of road. Stay left. Steep downhill past a few gates.

5.3 Go immediately left. View of dirt road that leads to Four Corners on opposite hillside (south facing).

5.6 Take a left on ST then a right on wide ST. Climb small incline up valley.

5.9 Go left across wooden bridge (Tenth Mountain Bridge). Four old wooden structures sit in the meadow ahead. Take ST heading left (to Four Corners road and away from the wooden structures).

6.0 Go right on dirt road up hill. Wooden fence along left side of dirt road. Head north. Views of the Maroon Bells behind you as you climb the dirt road.

7.2 Sunnyside Trail #1987 goes off dirt road (closed to motorized vehicles). Take the Sunnyside Trail.

(7.4) Take trail sign to Four Corners. Head straight uphill. Headed north.

(8.5) Four Corners. Follow Sunnyside Trail #1987 sign to left. Head west. To the east is Hobbit Trail. To the north is Lenado.

(9.1) Continue straight following Sunnyside Trail sign.

(9.7) Split in trail. Take left on Sunnyside Trail. Head south. Stay left on Sunnyside.

(10.2) Steep short hill.

(10.8) Continue on beautiful rolling singletrack through aspens. Glimpses of valley below.

(11.9) Sign for Shadyside to right. Stay on Sunnyside. Head west.

(12.0) Steep hill climb. Then no more climbing! The good stuff is ahead!

(12.5) Continue straight on Sunnyside. Shadyside comes in from right.

(13.5) Steep rocky downhill.

(14.2) Cross driveway or take the new crossing so as not to cross the land owner's driveway.

(14.5) Cross culvert. Follow arrows for trail. Steep. Steep. Steep.

(15.3) Hit road and parking lot.

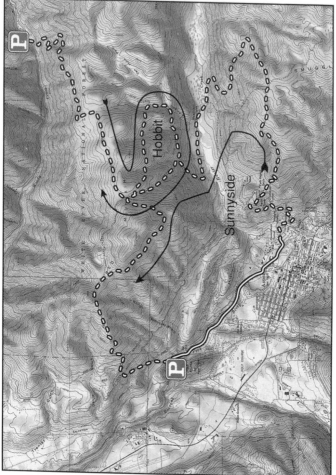

Elevation Cruncher Leg Burn Profile

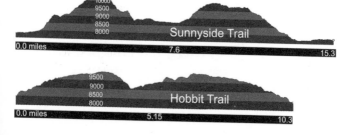

Hobbit Trail from Lenado

This is certainly one of the finest rides of the Western Slope. The singletrack on the Hobbit offers everything a mountain biker craves: tight turns, steep winding descents and incredible scenery. The Hobbit has sections so twisty that turns actually demand near-stops to navigate around aspens and pines. The open sections roar through beautiful meadows with occasional trail signs to aid the routefinding.

From State Route 82 take Gerbaz Road (4.5 miles up-valley from the Old Snowmass turn—a Conoco is on the corner) for 2.5 miles to Woody Creek Road and go left (to Lenado). Drive up Woody Creek Road for 8.0 miles to Lenado or, to extend the ride, stop at any number of pullouts before reaching Lenado.

Advanced. A few of the turns on the Hobbit require good bike handling skills. For the most part all hill climbs are fairly easy except for the pump in your legs.

1 hour to 2.5 hours

10.3 miles

5280'

Pitkin County #2, Aspen, Thimble Rock

If you do the ride in the summer or fall the flowers and aspens are incredible. This trail can be a mudbath after a heavy rain.

The Hobbit Trail mileage description

0.0 The 20-MPH sign just before the hill to enter Lenado.

0.3 Take a right on the singletrack just past the Welcome to Lenado sign. A sign for Four Corners is just up the trail. The ST turns quickly to a doubletrack with a loose hill climb. Head south and west.

2.4 A number of obstacles through rocks.

2.7 Veer right on doubletrack.

2.9 A distinct ST on the left (east) heads into the woods just before the flat section of Four Corners. A trail map is at Four Corners showing the Hobbit Trail. The ST from here is winding with some hill climbing.

3.3 Take a left at the ST intersection. Stay left at another ST intersection just after the first one. You will be on a well-traveled ST.

4.3 Trail begins to go down to Van Horn Park headed east.

4.7 Enter Van Horn Park. Hit Van Horn Park Road (a dirt doubletrack) and go right.

4.8 Take a left on the doubletrack. Great views of the ski areas around Aspen and Pyramid Peak.

5.3 Sign for Hunter Valley Trail #1992. Go right on ST and pass a couple of small boulders next to the trail. Head west.

5.7 View down to Hunter Creek valley.

6.1 ST dumps out on a road. Do not go left. Stay straight.

6.4 Sign for Hunter Valley Trail #1992. Go right on dirt road back to Four Corners.

7.4 Back at Four Corners. Head back down the trail to Lenado. The downhill is superb. Be aware of horseback riders and hikers.

10.0 Back in Lenado. Go left on road back to the 20-MPH sign.

10.3 End of loop.

Hobbit Trail

Buttermilk Trail

This memorable ride in the upper Roaring Fork Valley, offers a long climb, then some exquisite singletrack with great views from the East Summit of Buttermilk. As you crank, roll and fly along this narrow trail, you will be inspired by the panoramic vistas, which take in Highlands Peak, Pyramid Peak and Slevens Mountain. A major bonus to this ride is that it links up with the Government Trail.

From I-70, drive highway 82 up valley past the Aspen airport. Buttermilk Mountain (a large sign for the ski area) is a short distance past on the right. From Aspen drive down valley past the new turnabout and Buttermilk is on the left. Park here. The ride begins on the slopes of Buttermilk.

Definitely expert on two sections; a rocky stretch at the end of the climbing from the ridge leading away from the ski area, and the Governments' tree root section. Otherwise the trail is twisty, turning nirvana.

1 hour to 3 hours

11.5 miles

4640'

Pitkin County #2, Aspen, Highland Peak

An easy to ascertain ST trail after climbing the mountain. There is only one ST leading off the ski mountain and it meets the Government (one of the most-traveled trails in the valley). While on this ride, look around and enjoy the mountains, cliffs, and wildflowers. But be prepared for hard obstacles.

Buttermilk Trail mileage descriptions

(A trail map for Buttermilk is available at the lodge)

0.0 Start at the beginning of the steep Homestead Road located on the left side of the lodge at the base of the mountain. As the road turns away from the Summit Express lift, it changes to a faint doubletrack heading straight up Buttermilk. The trail described here ventures off the Homestead Road, but meets it again higher on the mountain.

0.5 Very steep hill (not the Homestead Road) following orange snow-making pipes on the right. This is the Baby Doe ski trail. Pass a green shed, covered with stickers, on right side of trail.

0.6 Trail sign on right for Drop Zone and Government.

0.7 Hit a dirt road and stay right, heading up the mountain.

0.8 Intersection with Homestead Road. Go left, heading south.

0.9 Brown gate and barbed-wire fence. Please close the gate.

1.0 Homestead Road sign on the right. Do not take the right hand road.

1.3 The Government Trail crosses the road just past going under the Summit Express lift.

1.8 Go past the Savio Lift and continue up, up, up.

2.1 Trail sign on right for Ridge Trail and Savio and Summit Express lifts.

2.7 Pass under Buttermilk West lift.

3.2 The East Summit at the Cliffhouse Restaurant. Continue on the Homestead Road up to the West Summit. A steep hill climb.

3.5 The top of the West Summit. Go behind the Warming Hut into the woods to an awesome ST that starts with yet another hill climb. Begins at numerous signs listing all the dangers to backcountry skiers. Head west along the ridge.

3.9 The hill climbing ends (but for a couple of minor climbs).

4.6 The last hilltop. The next section is a hike-a-bike unless you have many inches of suspension travel.

4.7 Barbed-wire fence. Go past on the ST and past a small pond to the north. This section may be cowed out.

5.2 Pass by a barbed-wire fence.

5.4 Intersection with the Government Trail. An orange gate blocks the trail going straight. Take a right through the rocky parts of the Government.

5.6 Cross through a small rock ridge.

6.0 Orange gate across trail.

6.3 Hit the first trail on Buttermilk. A sign with skull and crossbones marks the trail you just did.

7.6 Intersect with the Homestead Road and cross it on the ST on the opposite side. A sign for Homestead Road and Savio and Bear. The ST here is perfect. Options are to go down the Homestead Road, or ride STs linking the switchbacks in the Homestead Road, for a shorter loop than continuing on the Government.

8.0 The tree root obstacle. Then hit a dirt road and cross it on the ST. A left on the dirt road heads back to Buttermilk.

8.4 Sign for Eagle Hill. Stay left on the dirt road heading downhill.

8.5 ST continues on right of the road. A closed gate blocks the road. A wooden fence/maze must be walked through upon entering the ST.

(8.9) Hit a paved road and go left then immediately exit to the right on the Government Trail. A brown sign for the Government Trail may be on the right of the road.

(9.2) Wooden bridge on the right. Stay on the left side of Maroon Creek following a wide trail. Do not go left on the side roads. This trail eventually goes under Highway 82.

(10.3) Cross the Bob Helms Bridge, go under the highway and climb the steep hill that leads to the paved bike path.

(10.5) Take a right on the bike path and ride to the overpass along the highway. Go right on the bike path (across the overpass) and continue along the highway back to Buttermilk Mountain.

(11.3) Cross Stage Road and continue on the bike path. A small trail leads to the RFTA bus stop a short distance past Stage Road. Cross Highway 82 to the parking area for Buttermilk.

(11.5) End of loop in the parking area.

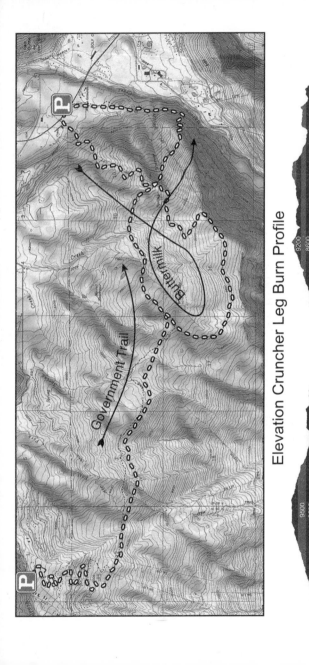

Elevation Cruncher Leg Burn Profile

Government

Government Trail

Oh, it doesn't get any better than this! If you live, breathe and dream singletrack the Government will satisfy any cravings. The short 2-mile hill climb at the beginning doesn't zap too much energy. You'll need arm strength, however, for clutching the brakes through the awesome singletrack that winds through Snowmass and Buttermilk Mountains.

From down-valley drive towards Aspen on Highway 82. Park one car at Buttermilk Mountain and then drive another car back down valley 0.2 mile to Owl Creek Road (a bike path follows this road all the way to Brush Creek Road). Go left and continue to Brush Creek Road. Go left and uphill to Wood Road. Go left then immediately right (sign for the Village Mall) then left into Base Lot A and park.

Overall advanced, but if every obstacle is attempted expert skills are needed. One severe drop through a mass of roots, some tight switchbacks and numerous water obstacles.

1.5 hours to 3 hours

12.8 miles for a shuttle
19.5 as a loop

2640' for shuttle
3240' for the loop

Pitkin County #1 and #2, Highland Peak, Aspen

A choice trail for testing speed on winding singletrack. Gorgeous wildflowers in the summer, and dramatic aspens in the fall. Well marked, and easy to find the right way since this is one of the valley's most popular rides.

Government Trail mileage descriptions

0.0 Leaving Base Lot A on the mountainside. Mileage begins under the wooden overpass above Wood Road. Climb up this paved road past multiple condominiums and trophy mansions.

1.0 Pass under an overpass just past Forest Lane. Stay on Wood Road.

2.1 Cul-de-sac at end of Wood Road. Take the dirt road leading left. Head east.

2.4 Gate. May be closed. Continue on dirt road across the ski slopes of Snowmass Mountain.

2.7 Alpine Springs Lift sign on left of road.

3.2 Sign for the Government Trail and the beginning of the ST. Take the ST downhill. Head northeast. Steep and windy. Expect rocky, steep water obstacles through the spring and summer. The beginning of the trail has red signs with yellow arrows, then after five miles look for blue diamonds.

3.6 Wooden sign on right with a skull and crossbones warning. Creek crossing immediately follows.

4.3 Red Government Trail sign on left of trail.

4.8 Split in ST. Take the right (more traveled) trail.

5.1 Creek crossing with wooden bridge. A steep hill climb follows.

5.8 Barbed-wire fence and red gate.

6.7 The first of three drainage and rock obstacles.

6.8 Orange gate on left. Stay on ST following the barbed-wire fence. Superb downhill section through a small rock ridge (northeast).

7.5 Orange gate across trail.

7.8 Hit the first ski trail on Buttermilk. A warning sign, for the trail behind, is on the right.

8.8 Orange water pipe on right.

9.0 Cross dirt road and continue on ST on opposite side. Head east.

9.4 The root obstacle! Then cross a dirt road. Continue on ST on opposite side.

9.7 Go left on road with the Eagle Hill sign.

9.9 ST continues on right of road. A metal gate may be closed on the road just past the ST. After getting on the ST, walk through a wooden fence.

10.2 Cross irrigation culvert with metal pipe. Then hit a paved road. Go left down to Government Trail sign and continue on the ST on opposite side of road.

10.6 Bridge across Maroon Creek. Stay left on trail heading north and follow the creek all the way to a highway overpass then climb a dirt road up to the overpass.

10.8 Green building on left.

11.7 Bob Helms Bridge. Cross the bridge and climb the dirt road to a bike path and go right towards the overpass.

12.0 Go right and cross the overpass on a bike path following Highway 82 down valley.

12.6 Cross Stage Road on the bike path.

12.8 Left on a stone walkway leading to a bus stop on Highway 82. Cross the highway to the Buttermilk Mountain parking area.

12.8 End of ride at the Buttermilk Mountain parking area.

19.5 For the loop to Base Lot A at Snowmass simply continue on the bike path, not crossing Highway 82 until Owl Creek Road (0.2 miles down valley). Climb the bike path back to Brush Creek Road to Wood Road and Base Lot A.

Rim Trail

The short loop is certainly well worth the trip. However, the extended loop ride is sweet, featuring almost eight miles of incredible singletrack with only a minimal three miles of dirt road, bike path and pavement. Added bonuses include great views of Snowmass Mountain and Garret's Peak, twisty singletrack through aspen and sagebrush, and numerous places to holler "this is awesooooome".

From down valley on State Route 82 go right on Brush Creek Road at the light to Snowmass Village. Drive past Alpine Bank and go left on Wood Road. Take an immediate right (sign for Village Mall) and then an immediate left into Base Lot A.

Advanced with steep switchbacks on loose dirt (both uphill and downhill). Most of the singletrack is near-perfect with an infrequent root or rut.

Short Loop—40 minutes to 2 hours
Extended Loop—1 hour to 2.5 hours

Short Loop—7.0 miles
Extended Loop—11.0 miles

Short Loop—1400'
Extended Loop—1600'

Pitkin County #1, Highland Peak

One of the best rides around for learning singletrack skills. Watch for hikers, especially on the weekends. The extended loop is in a Wildlife Sensitive Area, and is closed from September 15 to June 20.

Rim Trail mileage descriptions

(0.0) Base Lot A. Start the loop by exiting the parking lot. Ride out Wood Road to Brush Creek Road and go left.

(0.6) Right on Deerfield Drive. Locate the trail sign. Trail begins on left. Head northwest. Climb up switchbacks.

(2.0) Top of hill. Go straight past barbed-wire fence. Head north and east down winding ST. Do not take ST's going right or left at the barbed-wire fence

(2.5) Trail follows barbed-wire fence, on trail's left, along the ridgetop. Head northeast. Snowmass below.

(3.0) Take left trail.

(3.2) Barbed-wire fence. Go left on far-left trail.

(3.6) Barbed-wire fence on left of trail. Dirt hillside below.

(4.1) Rim Trail sign at split in trail. Go left up the steep hill. The Recommended Preferred Trail meets the left trail (0.4 mile) without additional climbing.

(4.4) Monster house on the left. Follow a faint ST on right of fence. Head northeast. A steep downhill with ruts meets the Recommended Preferred Trail then dumps out on a gravel road.

(4.7) Gravel road. Go right and follow the paved road down to Brush Creek Road. The Extended Rim Trail loop begins across the road.

(6.0) Cross Brush Creek Road and go right using the Brush Creek Trail to Owl Creek Road.

(6.3) Go right on Owl Creek Road.

(6.4) Go left on Brush Creek Road.

(6.9) Go left on Wood Road (just after Alpine Bank). Take first right (follow sign for Village Mall).

(7.0) End of loop in Base Lot A.

Rim Trail extended loop mileage descriptions

0.0 Begin as for short loop until mile 4.6.

4.6 Gravel road. Cross and begin the extended loop up a short steep hill. More hill climbing follows, interspersed between flat spots. Only open June 22 to September 14. Follow trails marked in blue.

5.9 Great view down valley. Start going down, down, down. Head northeast.

6.2 Go right following Hiking Biking Trail Only. Head south. The Rim Trail sign straight ahead should not be followed. The next section of ST is perfect! Pond and picnic table on right.

7.2 Hiking Biking Trail Only sign. Numerous trail signs follow this one.

7.9 Cross a wooden bridge.

8.2 End of Rim Trail with large sign. Go straight on gravel road headed back to Brush Creek Road. Head south.

8.2 Stay on bike path left of road.

8.8 Stay on bike path past a skateboard ramp and basketball courts.

8.9 Cross Brush Creek Road and go right on Brush Creek Trail along the golf course.

10.3 Right on Owl Creek Road. Go left at Stop sign on Brush Creek Road.

10.9 Left on Wood Road then immediately right (follow sign for Village Mall).

11.0 End of loop in Base Lot A.

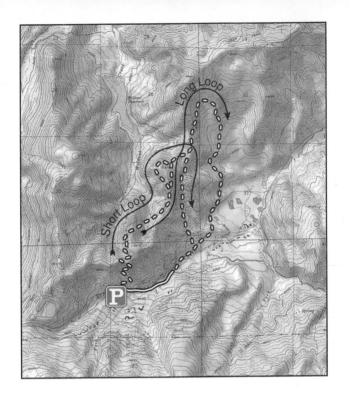

Elevation Cruncher Leg Burn Profile

Rim Trail- Short Loop

0.0 miles   3.5   7.0

Rim Trail- Long Loop

0.0 miles   5.5   11.0

Roaring Fork Valley

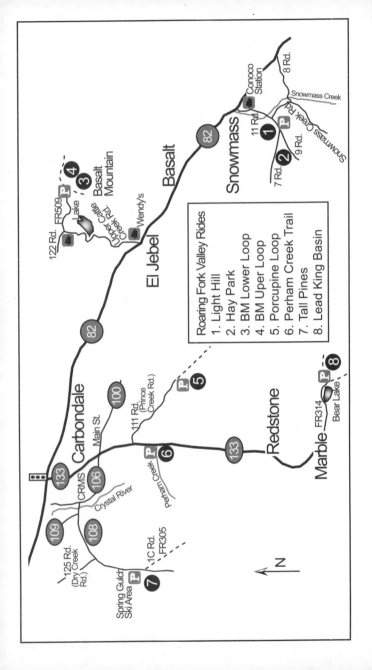

Light Hill

This short ride packs a wallop. The climb—a substantial one—meanders through a housing development before reaching a rutted and rocky doubletrack. This leads to an amazing view of the upper Roaring Fork Valley, with Mount Sopris and Capitol Peak stretching across the western horizon. The reward for the arduous hill climb is a terrifying descent down loose rocks, followed by near-perfect singletrack through sage. It is recommended that you maintain a speed which will keep the mind racing between fear and jubilation.

From State Route 82 (headed towards Aspen) take a right on Snowmass Creek Road (a Conoco station is on the corner). Drive to Gateway Road (1.3 miles) which is on the right after a bridge over Snowmass Creek. The best parking is found across from the Conoco at the intersection of Highway 82 and Snowmass Creek Road or at the intersection of East Sopris Creek Road and Capitol Creek Road (part of Light Hill loop).

Advanced to Expert, depending on one's speed. Can vary from reasonable maneuvering through rocks to spectacular feats of staying on the line.

Sub 1 hour to 2.5 hours

7.8 miles

2920'

Pitkin County #1, Basalt

This great training ride faces south, and is excellent early in the season. Expect rough (rocky) riding to reach the top of Light Hill, and on the beginning of the descent. The singletrack, lower on the loop, is fantastic. This trail is used by motorized vehicles so be careful.

Light Hill mileage descriptions

0.0 Intersection of Snowmass Creek Road and Gateway Road. Head up Gateway Road (a steep winding road) to a right on Light Hill Road at 1.2 miles.

1.9 A steep four-wheel drive road begins to the left of 0568 Light Hill Road. Head northwest. The road goes to the top of Light Hill alternating between road and doubletrack.

2.2 Stay right at doubletrack on left. Head northwest.

3.5 Overlook on left at a switchback.

3.7 Fence on left (made of sticks and green iron poles).

3.9 Go left past a fence opening. The trail descends from here. Head down the extremely rocky, steep trail to the south.

4.6 Take the right fork heading southwest past a fire pit (not up the hill with doubletrack). The ST ahead is all downhill, superb, winding and fast through sagebrush.

4.7 Take ST on right.

5.7 Hit a dirt road (East Cattle Creek Road). Go left. Head east. Stay left on Capitol Creek Road to Snowmass Creek Road.

7.8 End of loop at Gateway Mesa Road.

Elevation Cruncher Leg Burn Profile

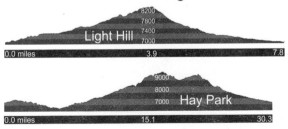

Ride map on page 40 with Hay Park.

Hay Park

This is undoubtedly one of the finer rides in the Roaring Fork Valley—a 30-mile loop that will satisfy even the most twisted masochist. A long paved and dirt road approach leads to a wide trail that eventually spits out on the Hay Park singletrack. After the uphill toiling, Hay Park opens up with superb views of Capitol Peak and Daly Peak.

Exit I-70 at Glenwood Springs and follow State Route 82 towards Aspen. Take a right on Snowmass Creek Road (a Conoco station is on the corner). Drive to the first Stop sign (1.8 miles) and take a right on Capitol Creek Road. Park at the intersection of Capitol Creek Road and East Sopris Creek Road at 2.1 miles.

Expert riding through drainages and creeks with a few sections of soft sand and babyheads. Most of the ride is bumpy dirt and nice singletrack.

2.5 hours to 5 hours

30.3 miles

4500'

Pitkin County #1, Carbondale 30x60 Minute, Mount Sopris, Basalt

The most spectacular view of Capitol Peak from any ride in the valley. Beautiful alpine wildflowers, an occasional water crossing (even in the summer months) and jaw-dropping singletrack.

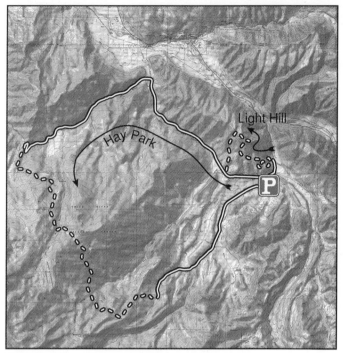

Hay Park mileage descriptions

0.0 Intersection of Capitol Creek Road and East Sopris Creek Road. Head west on East Sopris Creek Road (paved). Views of Daly Peak and the top pyramid of Capitol Peak can be seen to the south.

1.4 Road turns to dirt.

4.8 Road turns to pavement. Head northwest.

6.1 Go left on West Sopris Creek Road (paved). A reasonable angle of climbing with views of Mt. Sopris. Head west.

8.8 Road turns to gravel/dirt.

10.3 Sign on right for Sopris Mountain Ranch.

11.6 Take a right up steep switchback. Follow sign for Dinkle Lake. Head north.

(12.0) Left on dirt road headed straight toward Mount Sopris.

(13.5) Cattle guard with a wooden pen immediately on the left.

(14.0) Parking area.

(14.1) Trail leading off right with a forest sign about 50 yards from the road. Follow the wide trail (winds back and forth through the woods) up towards Sopris. An occasional loose section with rock obstacles.

(15.4) Metal gate. Please close it!

(15.6) Rolling trail section with a great view of the lower valley.

(15.9) Trail splits. Go left, taking the Hay Park Trail. Right goes to Thomas Lakes.

(16.3) Drainage with metal pipe.

(16.6) Pond on left.

(17.2) Creek crossing with two large metal drain pipes. Trail begins to have brief downhill sections.

(18.3) Barbed-wire fence with metal gate and cattle guard. Views of Capitol Peak, Daly Peak and Mount Sopris. A good place to relax. Beautiful ST follows with an occasional creek crossing. Head southeast.

(18.7) Barbed-wire fence with gate. Please close it!

(19.5) Steep hill climb.

(19.6) Top of hill with Capitol Peak in front of your nose.

(20.0) Another steep climb.

(20.4) Large creek crossing. Steep, difficult hill climb follows. At an intersection of two trails, take the left fork heading south.

(20.8) Another steep climb followed by the largest creek crossing.

(21.3) Cross another drainage.

(21.4) Woods open up with great views.

(21.6) Creek crossing with a man-made log bridge.

(22.9) Trail hits a 4x4 road. Stay straight (right) on road (left is trespassing). Head north.

(23.0) ST continues on right side of road then crosses it again to a ST on the left side. The ST here is steep and winding.

(23.9) Ride along a barbed-wire fence heading toward a dirt road.

(24.0) Hit a large parking area. Follow the road staying left, heading into the valley going down, down, down. Head north.

(25.6) Road is paved again.

(27.0) Big red barn on right. Stay on main road.

(30.3) End of loop.

Hay Park

Basalt Mountain - Lower Loop

This trail is a good mix of Forest Service roads and wooded singletrack. In autumn, the Basalt Mountain trail is covered in golden aspen leaves. This ride is at a pretty high elevation (8000'-9000'). Don't be surprised to find wet conditions in the woods.

From State Route 82 go east on Upper Cattle Creek Road in El Jebel (a Wendy's is on the northeast corner). Start mileage here! Drive up the winding hill into a housing development. The road turns to dirt and skirts a lake. Go right at 5.5 miles at a split (just after a house with a funky blue roof on the left). Take this road for another 2.2 miles to a large parking area with many roads and trails going every which way.

Advanced. A couple of water crossings may be deep and hard to get through. Most of the ST is easy enough unless you neglect to use your brakes.

45 minutes to 2 hours

8.8 miles

2200'

Leon, Carbondale 30x60 Minute

A great ride. Cruise this and you will be ready to step up to the plate for the double-digit rides. A good road to start and get the blood flowing. Beautiful fall foliage. Wet conditions and creek crossings exist year round.

Basalt Mountain Lower Loop

(0.0) Beginning of Forest Service road heading south from the parking area. Pass a gate, then wind your way up the gradual hill.

(1.8) Pond on left.

(2.7) A small flat meadow with 4x4 roads leading off to the right. Stay on the road heading northeast.

(2.9) Pass a gate. This will be closed during the snowy months. Continue on road keeping an eye out for the ST ahead and on the left.

(3.4) A faint ST dives off the road on the left. Head north. The ST is windy and "epic" on loam under large pines and aspen.

(4.4) Cross a drainage.

(5.0) Cross a large drainage/creek.

(5.3) Dump out in large meadow and hit a dirt road. Go right on the dirt road to a ST on the left of the road.

***For a shorter loop simply go left on the dirt road and follow it back to the parking lot.

(5.6) Take ST on left side of road.

(5.9) Ride across a big creek or cross upstream on logs. Go through a barbed-wire fence to the west. Head up ST to the north then follow the creek, heading west. Cross a couple of technical, wet ditches.

(7.8) Cross the creek and pick up ST headed left (south up valley).

(8.1) Barbed-wire fence and a log cabin off to the left. Hit the road and go right up a gradual hill.

(8.6) Pass by a gate (possibly closed in early season).

(8.8) End of loop at parking area.

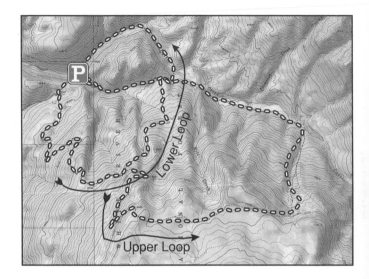

Elevation Cruncher Leg Burn Profile

Basalt Mountain Upper Loop

This extension of the Lower Loop is well worth the time and pump thanks to its extended downhill singletrack. Do the Lower Loop first to check for any springtime bogs. If the trail is wet and muddy, don't even consider doing the Upper Cattle Creek Trail. Wait till a couple of dry weeks have passed to set the trail up for better riding.

Follow the same directions as for the Lower Loop.

Advanced. The ride can be rather taxing with extended sections of rocky terrain at a high elevation (around 9500'). Most of the riding is reasonable singletrack through meadows and pines.

1.5 hours to 4 hours

15.9 miles

3700'

Leon, Carbondale 30x60 Minute

The trail can be very bumpy through basalt babyheads. Best to wait for the spring rains to diminish and for the trail to dry out.

Upper Loop mileage descriptions

(0.0) Leave the parking lot and begin on the Forest Road. Head south up the forest road, past a gate.

(2.9) Second gate. Closed to motorized vehicles through the spring.

(3.4) Lower Loop ST on left. Continue up the Forest Road heading northeast.

(5.2) Basalt rocks along roadside.

(5.3) Go over a cattle guard. At the top of the hill the road splits to the right and left. Stay straight. Head south and east.

(5.4) Gate and sign stating "closed to motorized vehicles".

(6.0) ST intersection. Sign for bikes. Go left. Head north.

(7.0) Go left on trail.

(7.2) Fence with metal gate. Trail is at times doubletrack.

(7.7) Large meadow initially surrounded by pine then switching to a large aspen grove. Take ST skirting through a couple of other meadows. Trail continues up a gradual climb past another large meadow.

(8.2) Tree with bike sign on it. Up gradual hill. Head south.

(8.4) Trail reaches top of hill. Head down through nice rolling terrain before climbing again.

(8.8) Trail heads back into woods from a meadow. Head east.

(9.1) Beautiful aspen grove surrounding trail. Blue triangle signs on tree. There are a number of creek crossings from 9.0 miles on.

(9.0) "T" intersection. Go left to Cattle Creek sign, heading north. Beautiful meadow ahead to Red Table. Trail goes downhill winding through woods and meadows.

(10.2) Barbed-wire fence with green gate. Black erosion retention pieces in trail through mile 10.

(10.5) Stay left. Main trail is steep and winding. Superb ST. Head west.

(13.0) Barbed-wire fence and an intersection in ST. Continue left. Head north and west.

(13.2) Go through gate and get on dirt road. Go left. Head west.

(13.4) Wooden pen on left of road.

(13.8) Stay left on road.

(14.3) Dirt road on left. Stay straight. There is a second dirt road on left. Stay straight.

(15.3) Cabin on right. This is where the Lower Loop hits the road that heads back to parking area.

(15.7) Metal gate.

(15.9) Parking lot. End of ride.

Porcupine Loop

The shortest ride in the book, perfect for the quick-fix junkie. This trail can be done on the spur of the moment and rusty skills can be honed on the bermed singletrack and rocky descent. One can extend the mileage by starting lower on the Prince Creek Road, or from Carbondale, to make a nice hour-long ride.

From the intersection in Carbondale on State Route 133 and Main Street (City Market on right), go south on Highway 133 towards Redstone for 1.7 miles. Turn left on Prince Creek Road (CR111). Park anywhere on this road or continue to the end of the pavement (3.2 miles). Park at a small pullout on the right just up from the beginning of the dirt.

Advanced with loose dirt sections, babyheads and sharp turns.

20 to 30 minutes
1 to 2 hours from Carbondale.

4.5 miles
9.4 miles from Carbondale

1000'

Carbondale 30x60 Minute, Carbondale, Mount Sopris

A better ride if one starts in Carbondale for a longer spin. Watch closely for the left turns (one for the ST and the last for the descent). The terrain tends to be rather loose and rocky. Great view of Mount Sopris.

0.0 The pavement ends, and the dirt begins, on Prince Creek Road. Head east.

0.3 Cattle guard.

0.6 Singletrack on left dumps out on Prince Creek Road. A metal gate is right of the trail. Continue up the road.

1.4 Campgrounds on right.

1.5 Take a left on a dirt road. Ride past a parking area, trail sign and gate.

2.0 Singletrack dives left off road. Head north and west.

3.3 Sharp left off the ST onto another wide ST. Head downhill (south and west) towards Prince Creek Road. The steepest section, and full of babyheads.

3.9 ST dumps out on Prince Creek Road. Go right back to the pavement. Watch out for cars on this road.

4.2 Cattle guard.

4.5 End of loop.

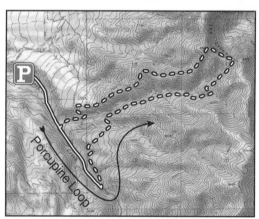

Elevation Cruncher Leg Burn Profile

Porcupine Loop

7500
7000
6500

0.0 miles   2.2   4.5

Perham Creek Trail

The Perham Creek Trail is an obscure trail in the Crystal River Valley, but the solitude and beauty of this ride shouldn't be missed. It originates just off Highway 133 in scrub oak terrain and ends in rolling alpine meadows with aspen groves. As with the Rim Trail in Snowmass the ratio of singletrack to road greatly favors the mountain biker. Every single inch of the trail is either singletrack, or doubletrack with one good line. Expect difficult climbing and a harrowing descent.

From the stop light on Main Street and State Route 133 in Carbondale, head up the Crystal River Valley towards Redstone for 10.2 miles on Highway 133. An unmarked right hand dirt/gravel road is on the right (two wooden poles mark the road). Not until exiting the highway does a sign indicate Perham Creek Trail. Park immediately after exiting the highway.

Expert. The climb is, without a doubt, one of the hardest around, dishing out challenges that include loose rocks, stumps and very steep climbs. The descent is a blast but wrecking in the wrong spot comes with a heavy price.

1.5 hours to 3 hours

8.8 miles

2300'

Carbondale 30x60 Minute

It is near impossible to get off the trail, as only one singletrack ventures into the mountains. Warm up your legs and lungs before venturing on this steep trail. The aspen groves and alpine meadows are not to be missed. Many possibilities exist to link into the Tall Pines trail.

Perham Creek Trail mileage descriptions

0.0 The beginning of the ST trail at the trail sign. Head west, up up and away. Perham Creek is left of the trail for the climb.

0.9 Great view of large sandstone fin right of trail. The trail heads down for a short distance.

1.2 You will be directly under the sandstone fin. Head west. The brush along the trail gets thick beyond with root and rock obstacles.

1.3 Cross a small drainage.

2.0 Trail begins to leave the creek and head north.

2.3 Entering a large meadow with aspens on the left. Trail is overgrown but discernible.

2.6 Intersection with another trail coming in from right. Stay left headed down.

3.3 ST on right of creek, heading down.

3.8 Wooden cabin visible in huge meadow across creek.

4.4 Barbed-wire fence and gate. Turn around and enjoy the awesome flats and descent down the Perham Creek drainage.
Option: Continuing past the gate and finding the connection to Tall Pines would make for a superb ride. Expect to carry the bike through Thompson Creek and adventuring on animal trails to the west to make the connection.

8.8 End of out-and-back at the Perham Creek Trail sign.

Elevation Cruncher Leg Burn Profile

Tall Pines

The Tall Pines trail ventures through the mountains just west of State Route 133 (leading from Carbondale to Redstone). The trail is mostly dirt roads with some superb singletrack to finish. The trail is substantial and very long, so most folks arrange a car shuttle to make the ride more doable. The entire loop is for the four-lunged biker. Some of the best views in the Crystal River Valley, particularly of Mount Sopris as it towers above you. Numerous cow trails intersect the main trail, so take your time with the route finding.

At the intersection of State Route 82 and State Route 133 take Highway 133 towards Redstone. At the Main Street light (City Market on right) in Carbondale (start mileage here) turn right and drive past CRMS (Colorado Rocky Mountain School) and across the Crystal River. Stay straight on the road up a steep hill and past the Crystal River Ranch. At 4.0 miles stay straight past Dry Park Road (RD125). At 7.2 miles a large parking area is on the right (Spring Gulch Ski Area—no signs). Park here or drive to FR305 on the left at 7.7 miles.

Advanced overall but expert on some of the steep hill climbs out of the drainages (easy hike-a-bike). Mostly reasonable singletrack without large obstacles. The final descent on the ST trail is a tad difficult.

1.5 hours to 4 hours for shuttle

17.9 miles with a shuttle between FR305 and Redstone. The recommended ride.
42.0 miles for the full loop.

4000' for shuttle
6340' for the loop

Carbondale 30x60 Minute

The ride is long so bring plenty of water and food. Expect to walk the bike as some of the hills are long and full of roots and rocks. Many downed logs exist through the first section of singletrack. Incredible views of Mount Sopris. If you do a loop it is best to get the hill climb to Spring Gulch and FR305 done first.

Tall Pines mileage descriptions

0.0 Start of FR305. A dirt road heads south and downhill. Stay on this road for numerous miles.

2.2 Camping areas on the right down by the creek.

2.6 FR305 crosses North Thompson Creek. A hill climb is ahead and leads away from the creek.

3.6 Top of hill climb. Sign on right for entering White River National Forest. Head downhill on FR305.

3.9 Intersection. Take the left fork to Thompson Creek. Right is for South Branch.

4.5 Cross a bridge across Middle Thompson Creek staying on FR305 through some switchbacks.

5.2 Mile marker 5.

5.5 Road sign for South Thompson Creek and Coal Creek. Stay left on the road away from the building behind the sign. Head southeast. The summit of Mt. Sopris is barely visible from the sign.

6.3 Road splits to the left. Stay straight, heading south.

6.8 Big red gate across road. Go through the gate and close it.

7.4 An intersection in road in a meadow. Stay left down a faint road that becomes obvious once leaving the meadow. Head south. Do not go through the brown gate to the right. Begin encountering ups and downs dipping in and out of drainages. These continue for many miles, unrelentingly!

(7.9) Head east down a doubletrack, with a drainage on the left.

(8.0) Cross the drainage and head up the doubletrack to the right with a mishmash of cow trails some aspens.

(8.5) Intersection along a barbed-wire fence on Parsnip Flat. Go through the gate and follow the South Thompson Trail #1952. A wide singletrack, along a fence, heads south.

(9.1) Trail crosses a creek and offers the first of three short, steep, hill climbs.

(9.4) Go through a silver gate along a barbed-wire fence. A trail sign is just ahead. A sign-in sheet is here. Please sign it so the Forest Service will maintain the trail. Follow the ST along the fence.

(9.6) Veer right on ST. Cross a creek and another steep hill. The hardest section to ride.

(10.3) The first of many more drainage crossings with steep hill climbs.

(11.1) Creek crossing followed by a wide trail through roots and rocks uphill to the pass.

(12.2) Top of the pass with a log fence of criss-crossed aspens. Sign for Trail #1952. The ST heads downhill here and is perfect. Do not climb any trails off to the sides of the main ST.

(13.2) Cross a drainage, with ST continuing on left side.

(13.6) Cross a creek into a large open meadow. When the trail "V"s, after the creek, stay on the right trail. Head south.

(14.4) Stay right on main ST at ST intersection.

(15.1) Go through a barbed-wire fence. Sign for bikers to yield to horseback riders. This section is very steep with many switchbacks.

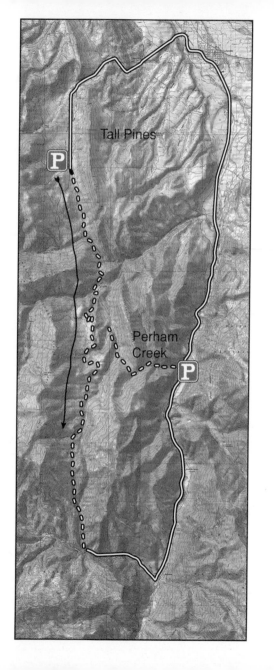

(15.3) End of dirt riding. Go to paved road (FR307) and go left back to Hwy 133.

(17.9) Intersection of FR307 and Highway 133. Go left back to Carbondale or jump in your car parked by the coke ovens.

(35.1) Main Street intersection with Highway 133. Follow Main Street past CRMS all the way to Spring Gulch Ski Area then FR305.

(42.0) End of huge loop at FR305.

Elevation Cruncher Leg Burn Profile

Tall Pines

0.0 miles   9.0   17.9

2 Locations in the Western Slope
Repair, Service, Selection and Supplies

LIFE CYCLES
Carbondale
La Fontana Shopping Center
(Hwy 133, near the railroad tracks)
(970) 963–BIKE

LIFE CYCLES, TOO!
Glenwood Springs
715 Cooper Ave.
(1 Block off Grand Ave.,7th & Cooper))
(970) 945–4FUN

Lead King Basin

The Lead King Basin trail is all four-wheel drive road. Now that you know there's no singletrack, it's time to reassure you that the ride is well worth your energy. Few rides get out in the mountains to the extent of Lead King and the ride is doable by everyone with a bike. As you climb the endless switchbacks found past Crystal City, in the back drop Snowmass Mountain and Capitol Peak rear their massive heads. Reason Enough!

From State Route 82 take State Route 133 to Marble. Go left on the road to Marble and drive 8.5 miles to the parking for Lead King Basin. The road winds through Marble (Park Street to Main Street) then turns rough for a short distance to the parking at the intersection for Crystal City and Lead King Basin.

Advanced. The road is very rocky through some sections and the down is rutted and very fast.

1.5 hours to 3 hours

13.3 miles

4600'

Carbondale 30x60 Minute

Beautiful! Watch out for the ever-present four wheelers. The exposure to lightning on this ride should be considered if the weather appears threatening.

Lead King Basin mileage descriptions

(0.0) Intersection of dirt roads. Sign for Crystal City 5 miles/Lead King Basin 5 miles. Take the right hand road to Crystal City. Head south.

(0.3) Lizard Lake. Stay right on the road and pass the lake.

(3.9) The picturesque Crystal Mine is across the river.

(4.1) Crystal City. Stay on the main road headed towards Scofield Pass. Head east. The road gets steep and loose.

(4.8) Go left at intersection in road to Lead King Basin (1 mile). Head north. The road stays rough and steep.

(6.0) Fork in the road. Take the left fork and pass over a creek and past a cabin. Head north.

(6.5) Fork in the road. Stay on the main left road.

(6.7) Cross a creek. The road begins to switchback—for far too long!

(7.7) Stay on main road. A road splits off left (do not take it).

(9.0) Intersection in road. Stay left. Head south.

(9.3) Stay left at the split in the road. Go down, down, down. Expect sharp turns, big bad ruts and awesome jumps.

(11.1) Intersection in road. Next to the road is a sign for Lead King Basin FDR315. Continue downhill. Head southwest.

(12.5) Big creek crossing. Take the right fork in the road just after the creek. Head southwest.

(12.9) Stay straight down the hill where the road splits right to the Colorado Outward Bound School.

(13.3) End of loop at Crystal City/Lead King Basin sign.

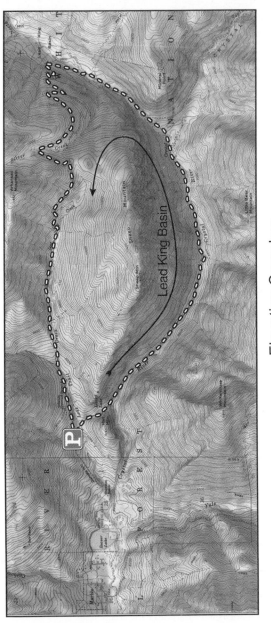

Elevation Cruncher
Leg Burn Profile

Glenwood
Springs

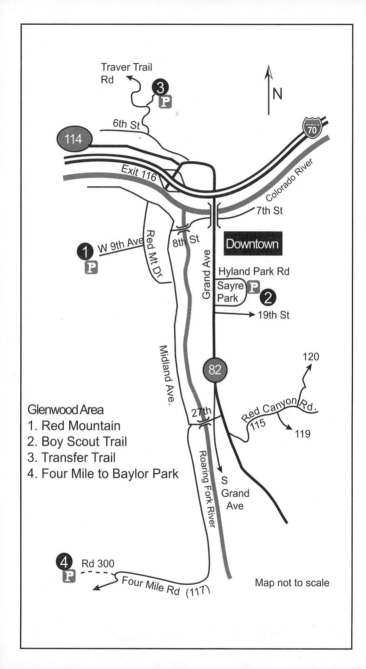

Red Mountain

Several of the rides around Glenwood Springs are steep climbs with blistering descents. This is one of them. The road was originally part of an old ski mountain that was turned into a park by the generous owner. An advantage to this ride is it is much easier than the Boy Scout Trail. A moderate hill climb that will get the juices flowing leads to a panoramic view of the northern tip of the Roaring Fork Valley and Glenwood Springs. The way down will bring smoke pouring from your brake pads and a smile to your face.

Red Mountain is visible to the west from anywhere in Glenwood and is west of the Roaring Fork River. From the heart of Glenwood head to the Colorado River (just under the overpass over the Interstate). Go left on 7th Street that turns into West 8th and cross the Roaring Fork River. Take a right on Midland Avenue then a left on Red Mountain Drive. Turn right on West 9th Avenue to a parking area for the Red Mountain Trail.

Expert on some of the ST, from butt-on-the-back-tire, to blue-knuckle braking. Up and down the road is easy.

45 minutes to 1.5 hours

6.8 miles with ST diversions
7.0 miles up and down the road.

3200'

Garfield County #5, Glenwood Springs

Do not continue through the gate (Private Property) at the top of the trail. The top of the trail stays wet as it faces north yet the rest can be dry. A good training ride for both hill climbing and descents. Offers a view of the Boy Scout Trail's descent across the valley to the east.

Red Mountain mileage descriptions

0.0 Parking area at beginning of trail. Follow the obvious dirt road to the top of the mountain.

3.5 Top of Red Mountain. A great view is seen from a rocky outcrop at the end of the road.

***One can return on the road for an easy descent or follow the directions below for some interesting singletrack.

3.6 Take ST on right of road, heading back east. The ST does one long switchback then meets the road lower down.

5.8 Take ST on right of road through some seriously steep ST. The riding through this section is extreme. The trail hits the road again. Continue down the road or take some final ST on right before reaching parking area.

6.8 End of loop at parking area.

7.0 End of out-and-back, if staying on the road.

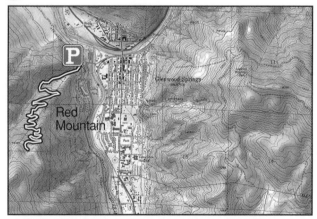

Elevation Cruncher Leg Burn Profile

Red Mountain

6500
6000
5500

0.0 miles   3.5   7.0

Boy Scout Trail

This must-do ride is certainly one of Colorado's finest. With a demanding hill climb from Glenwood Springs, quiet singletrack above Glenwood Canyon's massive limestone walls and a terrifying descent on perfect singletrack above town, this trail provides exceptional riding in a spectacular setting. The trail is easy to find, but once on it, a high degree of concentration is required.

Exit Interstate 70 (exit #116) in Glenwood Springs and go right through two lights following State Route 82 signs. Go across the Colorado River on Grand Avenue to Sayre Park (on the left past the downtown area and after City Market). Park anywhere at Sayre Park.

Expert at a high rate of speed. Numerous thin sections of singletrack offer potential for hazardous falls. Loose switchbacks and quick turns require excellent braking skills.

1.5 hours to 4 hours

19.4 miles

4700'

Garfield County #5, Glenwood Springs, Shoshone

The trail goes through a 4x4 area, so watch for motorcycles and trucks. Beautiful views of Mount Sopris and Capitol Peak before diving into the deep gorge of Glenwood Canyon. The trail above town can be full of hikers and bikers so be aware (it is tempting to go real fast through the bottom section, but this can be hazardous).

Boy Scout Trail mileage decriptions

0.0 Leave the Sayre Park to the north on Grand Avenue. Go to the second light and stay right (Sunlight Mountain) and get on South Grand Avenue.

0.6 Continue straight at the Stop sign. Do not turn right and cross the Roaring Fork River.

2.7 Hit Highway 82. Cross highway.

2.8 Get on Red Canyon Road (dirt road) and begin a very long climb.

5.5 Stay straight on RD115. Do not turn right on RD119.

5.9 Left on Lookout Mountain Road (CR120). Continue uphill to the north.

6.6 Split in road. Stay right.

7.6 Parking lot (big enough for 20 cars) on right. Leads to Forest Hollow Trail. Climb rutted 4x4 road to the northeast.

8.0 Road splits. Go straight. Do not go left. Follow brown trail sign.

8.3 Barbed-wire fence with metal gate. Keep heading towards the powerlines.

9.2 Haggard barbed-wire fence with trail sign. Continue under the power-lines down the hill. Still a 4x4 road. Head north.

9.5 Trail sign. Go left, getting off the 4x4 road, onto a wide singletrack. The trail gets good now.

10.2 Take obvious singletrack heading off left just past a marshy area. The ST dives into a winding, mostly flat section for a few miles. Head northwest then due west.

12.1 Technical spot with a bad fall. Trail crews regularly maintain this section.

12.8 Stay straight on ST. Sign on left for Glenwood Springs—5 miles, and Beer Creek—3 miles. Excellent view of Glenwood Canyon.

15.5 First view of Glenwood Springs.

15.6 Split in trail just after sign for Boy Scout Trail (on left before split). Head down hill to the right. The best section of the ride!

18.2 End of trail in a driveway. Trail sign with rules, etc. Take a right and go straight to Grand Avenue. Go left then ride until hitting Sayre Park.

19.4 Sayre Park and end of loop.

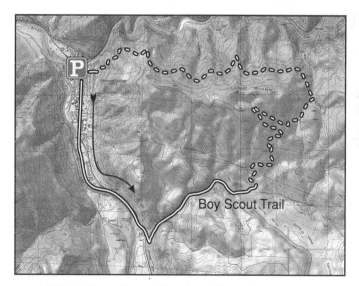

Elevation Cruncher Leg Burn Profile

Transfer Trail

The Transfer Trail is a four-wheel drive road that overlooks the confluence of the Colorado and Roaring Fork Rivers—and a brutal ride from start to finish. The redeeming qualities to this ride are torturous leg and lung burning as well as a terrifying descent over ruts, babyheads and loose terrain. Be sure to take in the great views and aspen-covered upper reaches of the trail. One can extend this ride by starting at the intersection of the Traver Trail Road and Transfer Trail, two miles before the normal start at the saddle.

From the main exit (#116) in Glenwood Springs, exit I-70 and drive to the first Stop light. Go left on 6th Street (Hwy. 6) headed west to Traver Trail Road and go right. Drive 0.4 mile to the sign for Transfer Trail. Go right up the dirt road for 2.0 miles and park where you overlook the mine, at the saddle in the road. The ride begins just up the Transfer Trail at the welded metal sign for the Transfer Trail. The trail can be seen going up to the east and the descent is visible on the south-facing hillside.

Expert. The sustained nature of the road (steep and loose) requires near-expert ability to complete the ride without coming off the bike. The downhill is very rocky and terrifying, and even worse after a rainstorm.

45 minutes to 2 hours

5.2 miles

3000'

Garfield County #5, Glenwood Springs

Bring along serious gumption if you want to ride the hill clean. Beautiful views of Glenwood Canyon and the Roaring Fork Valley grace this ride. The trail dries out early in the spring due to the south-facing exposure.

0.0 The start of the Transfer Trail loop at the welded metal sign for Transfer Trail-High Country Four Wheelers-Glenwood Springs.

0.5 Dirt road on left. Stay right.

0.9 Another 4x4 road on left. Stay straight. Head southeast.

1.0 Road goes left up steep, rocky section heading northeast.

2.0 Large meadow and a split in the road. Go left through the meadow and stay right when the road splits lower down (about 50 yards).

   ***One can also stay on the road and stay left when the road splits (up higher) to head back to the beginning. Another option is to take a right at the intersection to ride into the Flat Tops for some adventure.

2.3 Split in road. Go right on a faint doubletrack.

2.8 Meet the Transfer Trail again and go left. The ride continues downhill all the way back to the Transfer Trail sign.

3.1 Road on right. Stay left going down, down, down.

4.7 Meet main road that you climbed and go right. A trail sign for 602 is on the left of the road. Head west.

5.2 End of loop at the Transfer Trail metal sign.

Elevation Cruncher Leg Burn Profile

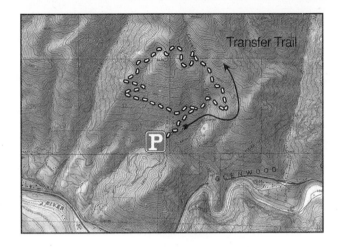

-preview other outdoor guides
-check for current inforamtion
-links to more trails

Four Mile to Baylor Park

This ride is primarily dirt road. However, some sections are singletrack, with miles of solitude and the chance to check out the mountains west of Glenwood Springs. As with many rides in the Flat Tops, there are abundant opportunities to veer off the beaten path, as cow trails and marked trails invite one into the boonies.

From Interstate 70 take the main exit (#116) for Glenwood Springs and head towards Aspen. Once on Grand Avenue, just after the Safeway, take the right split in the road following signs to Sunlight Mountain (South Grand Avenue). Go right on 27th Street (crossing the Roaring Fork River) following signs for Sunlight. 27th turns to Midland Avenue heading southeast. Follow the road as it bends right for Sunlight and take Four Mile Road (FR117) to the intersection for FR300 at the entrance sign for Sunlight. Go right on FR300 and drive 2.2 miles to a large gravel parking area on the left.

Easy. Only one long hill climb tests stamina and limits blood flow to the brain.

1.5 hours to 4 hours

23.6 miles

3250'

Carbondale 30x60 Minute

This trail follows frequented roads through meadows and along creeks. This is a great ride for previewing other adjacent trails. Check out Trail #2092 (at 7.80 miles) as a loop for a decent outing, but expect long cowed-out sections. The fall season brings orange-clad, gun-wielding men to the woods surrounding this ride.

Four Mile to Baylor mileage descriptions

(0.0) Parking area on FR300. Ride up, up, up FR300. Road signs abound for every intersection. Numerous dirt roads and singletrack/cow trails veer off the main road.

(0.6) Pass a cattle guard.

(2.4) Pass a metal gate and continue on FR300. Trail #2092 is on the left a short distance up FR300.

(5.6) The top of the hill. Cross a cattle guard, with a barbed-wire fence leading off both sides of road. Go down, down, down on FR300.

(7.8) Intersection of Trail #2092 and FR300. A good map marks all the alternative trails to check out.

(8.0) Intersection of FR300 and FR320. Stay on FR300. A pumping station is just up FR320 on the right.

(8.8) Cross a creek a couple of times. Head southwest.

(9.3) Intersection of FR300 and FR302 (to Baylor Park). Stay on FR300 (Haystack Gate–4 miles). The loop begins at this point.

(10.4) Go right to Haystack Gate.

(11.4) Intersection in a meadow. Go right to Baylor Park on FR300. Head north.

(11.6) Intersection of FR300 and FR302. Take FR302 (Baylor Park–2 miles) to the right. The road is less traveled through Baylor Park

LIFE CYCLES, TOO!
Glenwood Springs

(970) 945-4FUN

715 Cooper Ave.

Elevation Cruncher Leg Burn Profile

(12.8) Creek crossing to huge meadows.

(13.0) Intersection in the meadow. Go right following the brown 302 trail sign. A few creek crossings are ahead.

(14.3) Go left on FR300. Head northeast.

(15.5) Intersection of FR300 and FR320.

(18.0) Back at the top of the biggest hill. Head northeast.

(23.6) End of the loop at the parking area.

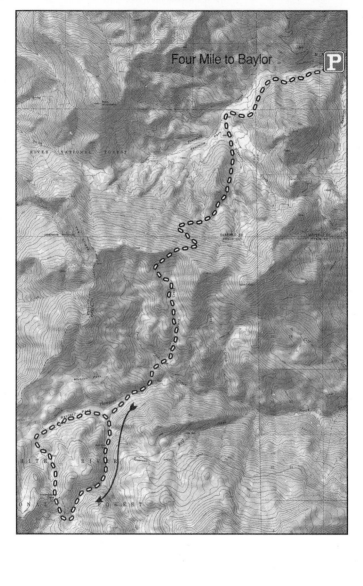

Four Mile to Baylor

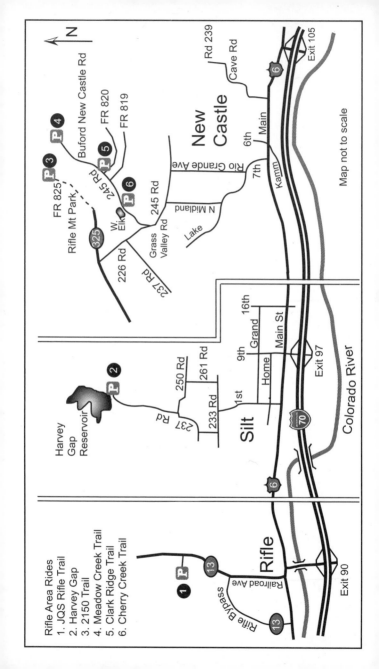

Harvey Gap

This new ride entails mostly dirt roads with an all-too-brief singletrack section before reaching the Grass Valley Road that loops around the west side of Harvey Gap Reservoir. The lower elevation of this ride (around 6500') makes this an ideal choice in the spring months when the high country trails are too wet.

Take the Silt exit (#97) off Interstate 70 and go to the Stop sign on Highway 6. Go left and drive 0.5 mile to First Street. Go right and follow the signs for Harvey Gap State Park. When First Street ends turn left on Silt Mesa Road for 0.6 mile. Go right on Harvey Gap Road (CR237)—many signs for the State Park lead the way—and drive to the parking area adjacent to the dam.

Advanced overall but some expert skills needed to get through the harder sections. The hill climbs on this ride are long and have loose sections on dirt and rocks. The descent from the Grand Hogback, with its ruts and babyheads, is frightening if taken at high speed.

45 minutes to 2 hours

10.4 miles

1250'

Garfield County #4, Glenwood Springs 30x60 Minute, Silt, Rifle Falls

First and foremost is the ride is new to bikes. The road is very rocky and picking a good line is difficult. A great ride in the spring.

Harvey Gap mileage descriptions

0.0 The reservoir dam. Head downhill on the pavement to the dirt road below the dam.

0.2 Turn right on the dirt road and immediately take the left split over the waterway in the road, passing two rusted farm machines. Climb a hill on the rough dirt road.

0.8 Top of the first hill. Road splits in both directions. Take the main road downhill to the northwest.

1.1 Go right at the split in the road avoiding the steep hill climb. Head north. The reservoir is down to the right.

1.2 Go left at intersection in two dirt roads, bypassing a steep hill climb. Head west.

1.3 Intersection on the left with the steep road that was previously avoided.

1.5 Start the biggest hill climb. Begins with a good line then gets rocky. Another hill follows.

1.8 Intersection. Stay right on a short downhill section. Reservoir is behind to the right.

1.9 Road comes in from the right. Stay straight.

2.2 Stay left at intersection. Head west. The Grass Valley Road can be seen below.

2.5 A sharp bend in the road to the right with a big cairn on the left. Descend the long hillside through rocks then it clears up to dirt.
*For more ST go straight uphill following cairns.

3.0 Four-way intersection. Go left, heading west, down more hills.

3.2 Pass a small pond on the left on a doubletrack. Head west then south to a wash.

Elevation Cruncher Leg Burn Profile

6700
6500
6300

Harvey Gap

0.0 miles   5.2   10.4

(4.2) Cross a big wash. Go right (northwest) down the doubletrack that skirts the wash. Do not climb the steep hill facing east.

(4.5) Start to leave the wash. A singletrack leads off right and requires ducking under a tree which overhangs the trail. A small cairn, marking the singletrack, may be present. The trail continues back to the wash through sagebrush. Grass Valley Road is visible at the beginning of the singletrack.

(4.6) ST crosses a steep drainage then continues on opposite side. Pass by a marsh on the right, then drop down into another wash and cross it to Grass Valley Road.

(4.9) Hit the Grass Valley Road and go right. A new barbed-wire/wood fence marks the end of the dirt riding.

(8.5) Go right following the Harvey Gap State Park sign on Harvey Gap Road.

(9.2) The north end of the reservoir. Sign for entering the park.

(10.4) End of loop at the dam.

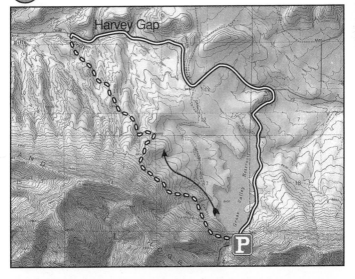

2150 Trail

The 2150 has to be one of the best trails on the Western Slope. Incredible singletrack follows Hoover Gulch and Three Forks Creek, past an abundance of beaver dams and creek crossings, and through some of the most pristine environments in the Flat Tops. This riparian ecosystem gives a dramatic contrast to the rolling terrain of aspen and spruce forest found on top of the Flat Tops.

Exit I-70 at New Castle (#105) and drive through town to 7th Street (CR245). Go right and follow the road out of town for 12.3 miles. CR245 turns to CR226 (Grass Valley Road) before eventually intersecting with State Route 325. Go right on Highway 325 until it turns to dirt in Rifle Mountain Park. Continue on the dirt road (FR825) into the White River National Forest. Park at the Spruce Picnic Area on the left. Check out GV Creek as an alternative.

Advanced. Difficult at times through the creeks and small drainages. Most of the singletrack is moderate with an occasional rock obstacle.

1.5 to 4 hours

18.6 miles

4175'

Trails Illustrated Flat Tops SW Rifle Gap, Garfield County #4, Glenwood Springs 30x60 Minute

The first 1.6 miles of the 2150 trail are difficult to follow. Keep a sharp eye out for brown trail signs after leaving the Bar HL Road. This is an excellent trail for wildlife diversity, a fact not lost on the hunters who flock to this area in the fall. Be particularly cautious during the hunting season as the Three Forks Campground and the Flat Tops are inundated with guns and RVs.

2150 Trail mileage decriptions

0.0 Intersection of FR825 and FR835 (Little Box Canyon). Go right on FR835 up Little Box Canyon to the Bar HL Road. Head northeast. A fairly grueling climb to the Flat Tops that follows the creek, until leaving it after 3.0 miles.

3.7 Steepest hill on climb to Bar HL Road.

4.3 Number of dirt side roads. Stay on FR835.

4.8 Intersection of FR835 and Bar HL Road. Go left heading north. Follow sign for Bar HL Park-7 miles.

 ***Do not exit the Bar HL Road until reaching the 2150 Trail.

8.5 Dirt road on right followed immediately by a pond on right.

9.1 Four Mile Road (FR214) on right. Stay on Bar HL Road.

10.6 Cattle guard.

11.6 Sign on right for Aspen Regeneration.

11.7 Three Forks Trail (2150) sign on left side of Bar HL Road. Sign is white with green and orange letters and highlights the ecosystem and points of interest. Cross through the barbed-wire fence and head left (east). Begins as faint doubletrack and fades as soon as it hits the aspen.

 ***The trail through the next 1.6 miles is not well traveled. Look for brown trail markers for 2150.

12.1 Trail marker, marked 150.

12.3 Trail marker on right of trail.

12.4 Trail marker on left side with no numbers. Mount Sopris can be seen at this point to the southeast. Begin a downhill section and look in the meadow on the left (east) for other trail markers.

(12.7) Trail marker with a 150 on it at the base of the meadow. Climb up hillside to the east

(12.8) Trail marker on left just over the hilltop. Begin a steep downhill section through an aspen grove. Another trail marker at the base of hill. Climb opposite hillside on obvious singletrack.

(13.0) Trail marker on right.

(13.2) A small band of limestone is next to trail with a trail marker just beyond. Head southwest.

*GV Creek goes left here to a pond then left on ST through a timber cut. Go past bulldozed trees (following cairns) to obvious ST (all downhill) that eventually meets 2150 lower. Bring Flat Tops SW Rifle Gap map!!!)

(13.4) Intersection in trail. Stay right and another trail marker is passed after approximately 30 yards. Trail at this point becomes clear and continues down on superb singletrack.

(13.7) Trail marker on left. Steep winding ST.

(14.2) Cross a small creek above beaver dam. Continue down along the creek on ST that occasionally crosses the creek. Do not exit on any of the side trails that leave the creek.

(14.9) Sign for Three Forks Trail, Beaver Gulch and Tangle Gulch. Cross to left side of creek.

(15.8) Sign for Trapper's Gulch on right next to multiple beaver dams.

(16.2) Sign on left for 2150. A steep trail exits to right (do not take it).

(16.5) Creek crossing with sign after creek for GV Creek and Irish Gulch.

(16.9) Sign for 2150. Stay right on main trail. Trail leaves creek to meet it later.

(17.7) Creek crossing followed by a barbed-wire fence.

17.9 Trail splits. Take a right and cross the creek on a red wooden bridge. Then go left on wide ST down the valley following the creek's right side.

18.4 Hit Three Forks Campground and continue down FR825.

18.6 End of loop. Intersection of FR825 and FR835.

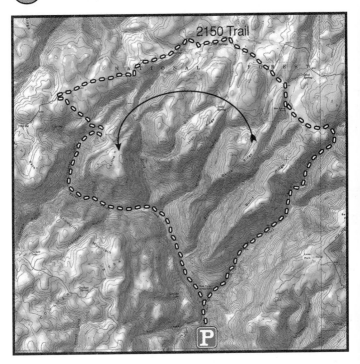

Elevation Cruncher Leg Burn Profile

Meadow Creek Lake Trail

This trail is mostly four-wheel drive roads and doubletrack. The best aspects are the spectacular scenery, easy-to-navigate riding, and a good all-around pump. As is the case with most trails in the Flat Tops, you will not get lost or have to bushwhack to reach Meadow Creek Lake. Once at the lake, many singletrack opportunities arise in the form of near endless trails or faint roads leading off into no-man's land. Check these out to further your adventure.

From the New Castle exit (#105) off Interstate 70, drive on Main Street to 7th Street (CR245). Go right and drive 5.1 miles to the Buford New Castle Road (CR245). Go right and drive 22.9 miles up on top of the Flat Tops to Fayville Jeep Trail (unmarked) on the right of the road. Fayville Jeep Trail is a doubletrack that heads into the woods. The Ute Trail is a good landmark, found directly before the Fayville, off the BNC Road on the right. The Ute Trail has a sign approximately 75 yards off the BNC Road just over a knoll (not visible from the road). Just over 2.0 miles past the Fayville Trail is FR601 that leads to Meadow Creek Lake.

Easy except for a couple of short steep, rocky sections.

1.5 hours to 4 hours

19.9 miles

2300'

Trails Illustrated Flat Tops SW Rifle Gap, Glenwood Springs 30x60 Minute

This is the safest trail to ride during hunting season as it follows mostly well-traveled roads. And it has the easiest route finding of any trail in the Flat Tops. The fall aspens and summer wildflowers are awe-inspiring.

Meadow Creek Lake mileage descriptions

(0.0) Intersection of Buford New Castle Road and Fayville Jeep Trail. Head north down the doubletrack of the Fayville Jeep Trail. Excellent rolling terrain that skirts the hillside.

(1.5) Cross a drainage followed immediately by two more.

(1.9) Road leads off right of the Fayville. Stay left on the Fayville. Head northeast.

(2.7) Intersect with FR601 (not marked). Go right on the well-maintained road. Head north.

(3.0) Stay right on the 601 at the intersection to Cliff Lakes. Do not take the next two roads that also lead off left to Cliff Lakes.

(3.4) Overlook to limestone cliffs and the South Fork of the White River to the north.

(4.1) Intersect with FR823. Go right and ride down to the lake. Head south.

(5.0) View of Meadow Creek Lake below to the south.

(6.1) Intersection of FR823 and FR821. Go right on FR821 and ride around the lake. Instead of merely following the directions below (back to the FR823 and FR821 intersection), ride one of the many singletracks around the lake.

(7.1) FR829 (unmarked) on left. Take FR829 and head east across the meadow.

(8.5) Pass by a couple of boulders in the meadow to the right.

(8.6) A faint doubletrack leads off left. Stay straight down the steep hill.

(9.8) Take a left on the faint doubletrack (FR649 and unmarked) just before the creek crossing. Head north on left side of creek.

(10.0) Pass a sign on the right for the Old Ute Trail.

(10.6) Go left on FR650 (unmarked). Climb the steep hill to the west through one difficult rocky section. The road splits left but stay right.

(10.8) Top of hill. A fire pit/campsite is on the right. Head west down a big hill.

(11.1) Old trail marker for FR650.

(11.8) Go right on road to intersection of FR823 and FR821. Head back out on FR823 to FR601.

(13.8) Go left on FR601. Stay on the road to the Buford New Castle Road.

(17.5) Go left on the Buford New Castle Road. Head southeast.

(19.9) End of loop at the intersection of Fayville Jeep Trail and the Buford New Castle Road.

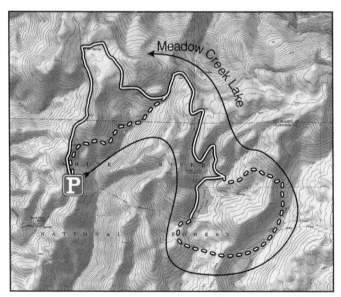

Elevation Cruncher Leg Burn Profile

The PATCHED TIRE

Bike and Skate Shop
Rifle, Colorado

Show this ad for 10% off products or services

We can fix anything.

We have great prices.

230 Railroad Avenue
Phone/Fax: (970) 625-6188

Clark Ridge Trail

The Clark Ridge Trail is the definitive obscure trail in the Flat Tops. You'll find plenty of adventure here as you follow poorly defined drainages, meadows and grass-covered singletrack. The lack of well-traveled singletrack lends an excellent quality of commitment. With the views, solitude and peace it is a trail not to be missed.

From I 70, take exit #105 into New Castle and drive through town. Turn right on 7th Street and continue out CR245 to the west for 5.1 miles. Turn right and drive up the Buford New Castle Road (CR245) for 10.3 miles to FR820. FR820 is just past FR819. Brown wooden road signs indicate both FR819 and FR820.

Expert on a couple of the hill climbs. You'll need serious skills and burly legs to pull off the creek crossing where the 2156 begins! The rest of the trail is moderate, with leg-burning ascents.

2 hours to over 5 hours

21.2 miles

3100'

Garfield County #4, Trails Illustrated Flat Tops SW Rifle Gap, Glenwood Springs 30x60 Minute

Trail-finding patience and skill is necessary for this ride. The trail is long and obscure, so bring a full assortment of orienteering supplies, plus plenty of water and food. Great views of the West Elk Mountains and limestone canyons.

Clark Ridge Trail mileage descriptions

0.0 Intersection of Buford New Castle Road (CR245) and FR820. Head north on FR820 downhill past a red gate.

1.0 Take a right on singletrack (marker for Trail #2291) before the second red gate. Pass a wood structure on left. Do not take trails that head off right a short distance past the structure.

1.6 Singletrack headed east above creek.

2.1 Barbed-wire fence. Marker for Trail #2156. Climb west-facing hill on opposite side of creek/drainage. Extremely difficult to ride as the trail is loose and rocky. ST heads east.

2.7 Overlook of Mansfield Creek and Clark Creek canyons. ST veers left headed north up Clark Creek. Stay on the upper trail as an occasional trail dives below.

3.6 Limestone cliffs are in the distance to the north.

3.9 Cross small creek. Head east.

4.0 Faint singletrack in meadow after crossing creek. Go right into woods. The trail becomes obvious within the trees. Head south up a continuous hill climb.

4.7 Trail begins to veer left heading north and east.

4.8 Trail convoluted. Veer right (south).

5.1 View of FR820 to the west. Trail is downhill at this point.

5.6 Meadow with the ST on opposite side. Head southeast.

5.9 "T" intersection in the trail. Go left (north) onto Clark Ridge starting in a trail/drainage. To the right is Clark Point. This is obscure! You are out in the middle of nowhere at this point. Choose wisely.

(6.0) View of FR820 to the west.

(6.9) Stay left at the fork.

(7.0) Small meadow with a view of FR820 behind and to the west.

(7.1) Hunting camp on right side of trail. Tire rim on the ground. View of West Elk Mountains.

(7.7) Down a small hill with a washed-out road on opposite hillside.

(7.9) Barbed-wire fence with a gate. Steep climb ahead veering a little left.

(8.2) Top of the hill. Panoramic view from Grand Hogback to the west to the West Elk Mountains and The Flat Tops to the east. Go right on wide, flat trail.

(8.7) Meadow with three short, wooden posts in ground. Dirt road ends in meadow. Follow road, which becomes faint, heading north.

(9.2) Closed Road sign. ST on left next to bulldozed road. Just after sign is a mix-master of dirt roads. Go straight out into the huge clearing to the north. Follow the main dirt road along Clark Ridge. Do not take any of the side dirt roads. Head north.

(11.7) Intersection with the Buford New Castle Road. Go left. Head west.

(13.4) Cattle guard.

(15.1) Intersection in road to Rifle Creek. Stay straight on Buford New Castle Road.

(20.6) Cattle guard.

(21.2) End of loop. Intersection of FR820 and the Buford New Castle Road (CR245).

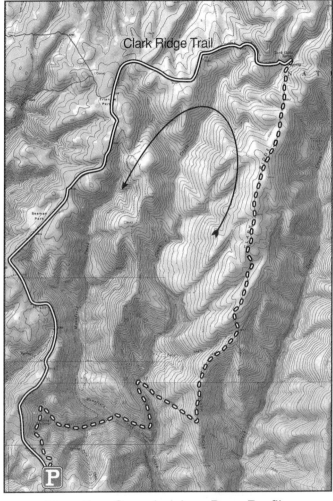

Clark Ridge Trail

Elevation Cruncher Leg Burn Profile

Clark Ridge

0.0 miles   10.6   21.2

Cherry Creek Trail

This is perhaps the quickest and easiest hill climb in the Flat Tops. The singletrack on the downhill is continuous, steep, clean and a real blast. Route finding is straightforward. One climbs up, then heads down, with only one small hill climb after the initial ride up the Buford New Castle Road.

Take the New Castle exit (#105) and drive through town to 7th Street (CR245). Go right and follow the road out of town (for 5.1 miles) and turn right on the Buford New Castle Road (still CR245). Drive up the road to the White River National Forest sign (4.2 miles and a cattle guard) and park or drive another 0.4 mile to a left-hand dirt road for additional parking.

Advanced. Expect an occasional blind turn with a rock and muddy sections. Creek crossings are rocky with thick mud sides. A good trail for improving one's speed and efficiency.

1 hour to 3 hours

12.0 miles

4480'

Trails Illustrated Flat Tops SW Rifle Gap, Garfield County #4, Glenwood Springs 30x60 Minute

Hunting season in the Flat Tops is a major issue (either ride on a well-traveled trail—this isn't one of them—or wear very bright colors and make a lot of noise). This trail has some of the best views of the West Elk Mountains from anywhere in the Flat Tops. Keep in mind the trail may be cowed out!

Cherry Creek Trail mileage descriptions

Begin ride at parking area at White River National Forest sign (1.0 mile to Cherry Creek Trail sign) or up the road in the left-hand pullout (0.6 mile to Cherry Creek Trail sign).

(0.0) Intersection of Cherry Creek Trail and Buford New Castle Road. Sign for Cherry Creek Trail and trail marker for Trail #2292. Head north up the road for several miles.

(6.8) Take a right on FR819. Head east on a 4x4 road.

(7.3) Barbed-wire fence lining the left side of road.

(7.5) Stay straight when a road splits off right. Pass a cattle pen found just below a short hill climb ahead.

(7.8) Barbed-wire fence/gate at top of the hill. Keep the gate closed. Go right on doubletrack to the southwest. Awesome view of the West Elk Range to the southeast.

(8.0) Barbed-wire fence on right and a gate. Stay left on ST along the fence going downhill. Continue along the fence that has green and orange stakes.

(8.7) Leave the barbed-wire fence and go left on ST. Head southeast along a steep drainage. The trail peters out in a meadow at the base of the hill. Stay left of a barbed-wire fence and cross a small creek.

(9.0) Take a right through a barbed-wire fence/gate. Follow Trail #2292. From here on, stay next to creek. Head south and east. Do not leave the creek on any of the STs that head up the hillsides.

(9.1) Trail #2292 sign. Trail improves dramatically further down the creek.

9.8 Barbed-wire fence/gate. Please close this gate to keep cattle off the upper trail. Stay on trail following drainage. Do not go up steep trail on left. Perfect ST below with limestone cliffs above on upper left hillside.

11.5 Intersection with wide trail. Stay left.

11.9 Slickrock and loose dirt section. Stay left at any divergence to the right (these are made by cattle leaving the main trail).

12.0 End of loop at Buford New Castle Road. Ride down to the parking.

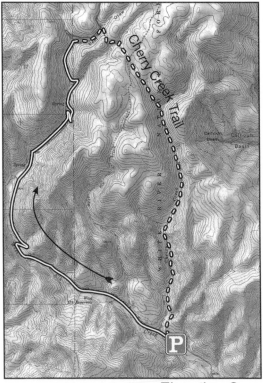

Elevation Cruncher
Leg Burn Profile

Cherry Creek

| 8000 |
| 7500 |
| 7000 |
| 6500 |

0.0 miles   6.0   12.0

JQS - Rifle Trail

This ride is more of an obstacle course than a cruiser classic, yet it does offer some quality singletrack. What the JQS Trail lacks in aesthetic beauty it quickly makes up for in fun (and pain) by frequent twisting, turning, climbing and dropping. The descents are fun, but they are usually followed by an abrupt and steep climb. The trail is shared by motorcycles so keep in mind that a 200 pound machine could whip around the next corner.

From Interstate 70 take exit #90 for Rifle. Drive through town on Railroad Avenue. Then right on US Route 13 towards Meeker. A short distance on the right is Fireside Lanes. Drive 0.2 mile past the Fireside Lanes on US Route 50. Turn left on an obscure dirt road that drops down a hill and crosses a wash. Continue uphill on the road for 0.5 mile and park on the left or right.

Expert (the trail was originally made for machines with 60 horsepower).

45 minutes to 2 hours

8.3 miles

Unknown. The trail goes up and down nearly a hundred times.

Garfield County #4, Glenwood Springs 30x60 Minute, Rifle

Try to ride the trail mid-week, when the motorcycles are few and far between. Besides the obvious roller coaster riding, heading every which way, be aware of soft sand in the washes. Bring plenty of water (this is a lot of work for a short trail). Longer loops abound for the enthusiastic rider.

JQS – Rifle Trail mileage descriptions

0.0 Ride west on the dirt road following the power-lines. Do not exit on left roads.

0.5 Cattle guard across dirt road.

0.6 Singletrack on left heads southeast—then west—then back northeast—then west again—on rolling singletrack.

1.7 Trail comes within view of dirt road and follows it on the left.

2.3 Trail dumps out on dirt road. Go left and stay on road. A singletrack does exit the road on the left and eventually meets back with the road.

2.6 Stay left. Do not take right road.

2.7 Take a left on a dirt road heading south then back on singletrack just left of road.

2.9 Overlook, just off the singletrack (fire pit in area). Stay on singletrack (with a green barbed-wire fence on the left after the overlook).

3.0 A long section of supreme roller coaster riding heading primarily to the west.

4.6 Road is visible to the right.

4.9 Singletrack is visible in the canyon below.

5.0 A hairpin turn descends into canyon and across a couple of washes. Two trails, one from the north and one from the west, converge in the last wash.

5.2 Leave the wash and head east.

5.4 Continue east past a singletrack coming down the hill to the right.

5.7 Go through a haggard barbed-wire fence. Immediately turn left, through the wash (trail non-existent near fence), then right on doubletrack heading east again. The fence continues up the hillside to a mud cliff.

6.1 Cross a downed barbed-wire fence on singletrack. Go left (northwest). This is the most technical section of the ride with washes and deep ruts on steep climbs.

6.9 Fence on left. Follow the trail along the fence, heading east.

7.3 Top of a steep hill. Go down a steep descent.

7.5 Intersection (wide motocross trail). Go left. Powerlines are visible on the hillside to the northeast.

7.7 Dirt road. Go right. Cattle guard on left.

9.3 End of loop at parking area.

Elevation Cruncher Leg Burn Profile

**BMX
Road
Mountain**

**Mountainbike
Rentals &
Demos**

**Lifetime
Service
Guarantee**

**Layaway &
Financing**

*BICYCLE
OUTFITTERS*

**251 Colorado Avenue
Grand Junction
970-245-2699**

TREK

GT

KLEIN
Handcrafted Science™

Jamis

Grand Ave.

340

50

2nd

Main

3rd St.

5th St.

Colorado

Grand Junction
Fruita

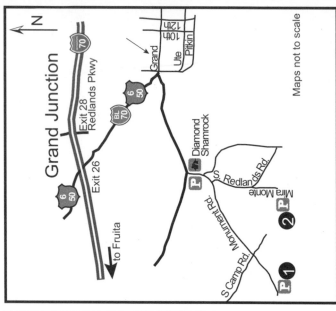

Grand Junction

N ←

Exit 28
Redlands Pkwy

Exit 26

to Fruita

Diamond Shamrock

P

S. Redlands Rd.

Mira Monte

S Camp Rd.

S Monument Rd.

Grand

Ute

Pitkin

10th

12th

P 2

P 1

Maps not to scale

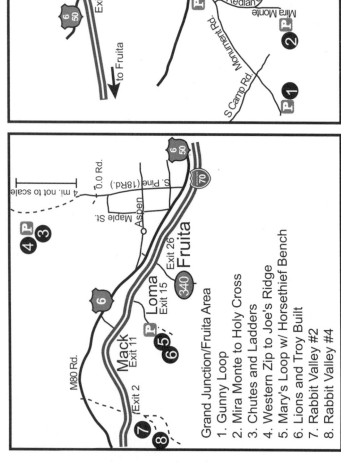

4 mi. not to scale

S. Pine (18Rd.)

0.0 Rd.

Maple St.

Aspen

P 4 3

M80 Rd.

Mack
Exit 11

Loma
Exit 15

Fruita

Exit 26

340

(Exit 2)

P 5

6

7

8

Grand Junction/Fruita Area

1. Gunny Loop
2. Mira Monte to Holy Cross
3. Chutes and Ladders
4. Western Zip to Joe's Ridge
5. Mary's Loop w/ Horsethief Bench
6. Lions and Troy Built
7. Rabbit Valley #2
8. Rabbit Valley #4

Gunny Loop

A classic ride whose scenery comes alive after leaving the initial Lunch Loop Area. Frequented by hordes of bikes, trucks and motorcycles, the options to get off trail are vast. A bike computer will help you navigate the trail more easily unless getting off the so-called beaten path is your bag.

From Interstate 70 in Grand Junction take Exit #26. Go left on US Route 6/50 then left on Broadway (near City Market), following the signs for Colorado National Monument. Take a left on Monument Road (at the Diamond Shamrock station) just after crossing the Colorado River. Drive 2.0 miles to the trailhead on the left for the Tabeguache Trail.

Advanced on some of the singletrack sections but easy other than the leg pump

1.5 to 3 hours

9.0 miles

4000'

Colorado National Monument

The area is a mess from over-zealous motorized vehicles, so be patient deciding on which way to go. The views of the Monument are inspiring with the funky-shaped rocks and weird dirt. Check out the BLM map to get your bearings if necessary.

Gunny Loop mileage descriptions

0.0 Head south up wash.

0.5 Take right fork up a steep 4x4 hill following Tabeguache Trail.

1.5 Stay straight up steep hill on main 4x4 road with small slickrock sections. Do not take right (headed west) for Eagles Wing portion of loop.

2.0 Continue south on 4x4 road to Little Park Road.

2.5 Turn right on pavement up a hill and continue to Little Park Staging Area on left.

2.8 Do not take ST for The Ribbon Trail on right.

3.1 Little Park Staging Area on left. Continue through gravel parking area. Road veers to the right (avoid the spur on the left) and continue on good gravel road. Keep an eye out for Gunny Loop sign and a cairn and take a left. The road peters out at a fire ring, continue on doubletrack.

4.2 Go left on a ST (Bike Peddler volunteer sign here). The ride improves drastically here, as the ST is awesome with some serious technical sections. The ST through the valley lasts over 2.5 miles.

6.8 Hit Little Park Road. Cross the road to ST on opposite side to Lower Gunny Loop.

7.2 Go left at junction across a hillside to a steep hill climb.

7.4 Trail turns to doubletrack and heads uphill and left. Climb a technical hill to a rocky ridge.

7.6 Take a right at junction.

8.0 Go straight to a short hill.

8.3 Go left down a steep bentonite clay hill (cairn at the top).

9.0 End of loop to parking area.

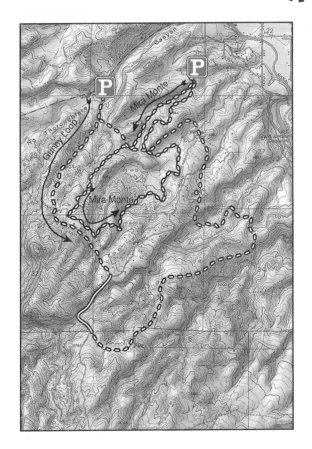

Elevation Cruncher Leg Burn Profile

Get Service Not attitude!

CYCLERY & DIVE CENTER

GARY FISHER
LEMOND
MONTY
HARO

**657 North Avenue
Grand Junction
(970) 245-7127**

Mira Monte to Holy Cross Loop

The Mira Monte and Holy Cross Loop combines exquisite desert scenery, tight singletrack, and a plethora of obstacles that will test your technical riding skills. Consider riding this loop more than once, as what seems improbable may become rideable.

From Interstate 70 in Grand Junction take Exit #26. Go left on US Route 6/50 then left on Broadway (near City Market), following the signs for Colorado National Monument. Take a left on Monument Road (at the Diamond Shamrock station) just after crossing the Colorado River. Park across from the Shamrock in the big parking lot (1.0 mile from trailhead). Do not park at the small private trailhead proper. Instead, get on your bike here and head up Monument Road taking the first left onto Redlands Road. At 0.7 mile from the Shamrock, Redlands Road meets Mira Monte Rd. Go straight on Mira Monte instead of curving left on Redlands. The pavement soon turns to dirt and a dirt parking area and trailhead are apparent. (Again, don't park here. This is private property)

Some expert moves—with advanced areas in between

1 to 2.5 hours

5.8 miles

460'

Colorado National Monument

Keep your eye out for the trail's namesake - a wooden cross. Many side trails await exploration. New spur trails constantly appear so stay on the main trail if in doubt.

Mira Monte to Holy Cross mileage descriptions

(0.0) Begin mileage from where the singletrack meets the parking area. Trail heads south/southwest. Stay on main trail and relax during these less technical moments and fine scenery.

(1.1) Go right at this major fork in the trail.

(1.3) Stay left at fork, and continue up steep hill.

(2.0) Take the left fork and carry your bike through the narrow Lemon Squeezer section. The right fork hooks up with the Tabeguache Trail.

(2.2) Fork in trail with a large boulder on right. Stay left.

(2.3) A rock fin marks the next important intersection with the Tabeguache Trail. Do not continue straight up the Widowmaker hill. Turn left onto the Holy Cross Trail. Cruise down a mild-looking field. Things heat up in a hurry from here.

(4.4) After a technical trip across a rock ridge the ride enters another pleasant meadow.

(4.7) Go right at intersection

(5.6) Go right at intersection

(5.8) Return to dirt lot at the beginning of the Mira Monte Trailhead.

Refer to map for Gunny Loop page 103.

Elevation Cruncher Leg Burn Profile

Chutes and Ladders

It won't take you long to figure out how this trail got its name. A continual need to crank then brake defines this ride. After the initial ups and downs, the trail dumps out on the plain below the Book Cliffs and provides more great singletrack. A superb ride with challenges for beginners riders to experts.

Follow directions for Western Zip to Joe's Ridge.

All over the place but tending toward very advanced. Some of the hill climbs are very steep and loose.

30 minutes to 1.5 hours

7.0 miles

700' at least. Far too many ups and downs to get a perfect count.

Mesa County #1, Ruby Lee Reservoir

An easy trail to discern. There is a great beginning to the ride before the Chutes and Ladders hit you in the face. Try to get on this trail mid-week, the weekend hordes can be as thick as flies on a carcass.

Chutes and Ladders mileage descriptions

0.0 Parking lot. Cross 18 Road heading northeast to a ST heading down a steep hill. Hit a pond surrounded by a mix-master of trails. Go left (north) on a double ST towards the Book Cliffs. Trail follows a drainage and parallels 18 Road.

1.3 Split in ST. Go right past a pond/marsh with a closed road along its south side. An obvious singletrack heads north. Excellent small ups and downs and rock obstacles.

2.2 Split in trail. Chutes and Ladders goes right up two very steep hills. Frontside Trail goes left. After the hills, the trail heads east through multiple gullies and drainages along the base of the Book Cliffs. Expect to hill climb some more through the next half mile.

2.9 Hit a drainage followed by a steep climb out.

3.2 Trail begins to go down, down, down to the southeast. The best part of the ride.

3.5 Trail crosses a doubletrack. Stay on the trail. Trail follows an irrigation ditch on superb ST.

4.1 Dirt road on right.

5.0 Take a left on dirt road to the corral (orange and wood stakes). Go right at the corral (southwest) on a wide ST.

5.7 Trail crosses a doubletrack and many wide, flat drainages toward a valley to the west. Once you drop into the valley, follow the left ST (headed southwest).

6.2 Hill climb on east face to exit the valley. Head west.

6.3 Parking lot visible to the west.

6.8 Back at pond below 18 Road and the parking lot. Climb the hill to the west to reach the parking lot.

7.0 End of loop at the parking lot.

Chutes and Ladders

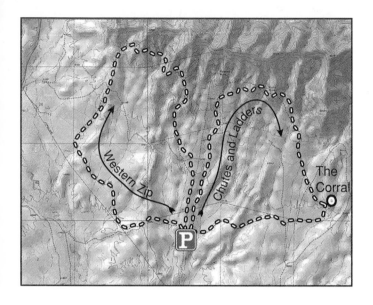

Elevation Cruncher Leg Burn Profile

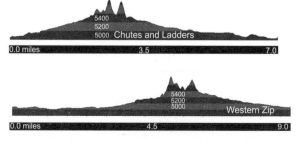

Western Zip to Joe's Ridge

As with any ride at the Book Cliffs, one can ride a multitude of directions and yet end up back at the parking area. The Zip to Joe's Ridge takes in two of the nicer sections of singletrack while bypassing the ever popular Prime Cut section that leads to the Frontside or Chutes and Ladders. This ride offers a number of difficulties. There are steep hillsides to climb, and abrupt drainage crossings that can grab a front wheel like a vice. One of the many great benefits of this ride is easy route finding, a meager elevation of 4500', and awesome winding singletrack.

From Interstate 70 take the Fruita exit (#19). Go right from the off ramp and then right at the Stop sign (Burger King is immediately across the road). Follow this around the Park Square and then right on Aspen Street (Over the Edge Sports is one block down on the right). Follow Aspen Street to Maple Street and go left. Drive to N 3/10 Road (just past Road M) and go right. Go left at a T intersection on 18 Road. The road turns to dirt (stay on the main dirt road), and the parking area is just over 4.0 miles on the left (marked by rocks around the lot).

Expert on the steep loose hill climbs. Most of the riding goes up and down small ridges with an occasional drainage crossing. Expect to walk the bike a little.

45 minutes to 1.5 hours

9.0 miles

900' at least. The trail goes up and down too many times to get a good count

Mesa County #1, Ruby Lee Reservoir

Superb riding in every season but summer. The fall and winter conditions are excellent. Expect hefty crowds on the weekends. A good ride to get the lungs in shape for higher elevation rides.

Western Zip mileage descriptions

0.0 From the parking area, head southwest on the singletrack. The ST dips down to a barbed-wire fence.

0.3 Cross the fence and climb a couple of short steep humps to the west.

0.7 Go left at a T intersection in the ST. A small wooden block with a tire points left. Head south.

1.3 Go right on the dirt road. Follow the road right of the power lines. Head west.

2.1 Road splits. Stay right.

2.9 A ST leads off the road on the right. Cairns may mark the ST. Head northwest.

3.5 Pass through a barbed-wire fence and gate. Close the gate. Head north towards the Book Cliffs.

3.9 Faint ST leads off right. Stay left on the well-traveled leftmost ST.

4.3 Cross a dirt road and continue on ST on opposite side.

4.7 Go right at intersection in ST. Head back east along the base of the Book Cliffs.

5.4 At base of drainage go left. This is a hike-a-bike section. Head east to the trail easily visible on the west face.

5.6 Top of hill. Head south along the ridgeline. Head down to the east after a closed section of the trail on the right.

6.1 Climb a couple of steep hills.

6.7 Trail cuts back right to the south, and follows the right side of a drainage.

6.8 Intersection in ST. Joe's Ridge goes right up a small hill to the ridgeline. Best part of the ride.

7.6 Trail turns to doubletrack.

7.9 Trail hits a dirt road. Go left.

8.2 ST leaves road on right.

8.5 ST hits 18 Road. Go right back to parking area.

9.0 End of loop at the parking lot.

Western Zip

Mary's Loop w/ Horsethief Bench

Undeniably one of the best rides in Fruita. The easy going trail affords the opportunity for beginners as well as advanced riders to enjoy an awesome trail with scenic views of the Colorado River and surrounding sandstone canyons. Expect all kinds of trail, from cruiser doubletrack to hiking on one short section.

From Interstate 70 take the Loma exit #15. Drive on the south frontage road toward the Weigh/Check Station. Go left on a dirt road before entering the Weigh Station and drive 0.6 mile to a large parking area on the right with a map for the MTB rides.

Advanced. Riding down to reach Horsethief Bench is the only real difficulty.

13.0 miles

1.5 hours to 3 hours

1700'

Mesa County #1, Mack

A great ride. Best during the week, as Fruita rides have become very popular with the weekend warriors. Bring plenty of water and a shell for the possible changes in desert temperatures. Pretty damn hot in the middle of summer.

Mary's Loop mileage descriptions

0.0 Parking area. Head up the short hill to the south.

0.5 Go right (west) on the hill climb starting Mary's Loop. The third dirt road on the right after the hilltop above the parking area.

1.9 Overlook.

2.0 Go left down the extremely technical cliff to start Horsethief Bench.

2.1 Split in the trail. Go left (south and east) on excellent ST. The trail heads back west above the Colorado River. Expect a few technical spots.

3.9 Head back north out of a small drainage/wash going uphill. A sign is in the wash.

5.1 At "Y" intersection, follow the right drainage. This follows the base of a cliff back east through infrequent washes to the start of Horsethief Bench. Be mindful that the trail gets washed out after rain. The technical cliff band can be seen on the last part of the Bench loop.

6.1 Back at the top of the cliffband. Go left and continue on Mary's Loop.

7.4 Kokopelli Trail Map on right of trail.

8.0 Steep, short hill with two rock steps to reach more flats.

8.7 Steve's Loop start on left.

9.7 Steve's Loop exit on left.

9.9 Go right for the end of Mary's Loop (headed north and west). Left is the beginning of Lion's Loop to Troy Built.

10.4 Top of hill with a cattle guard.

10.5 Hit the dirt road and go right back to parking area.

13.0 End of loop at parking area.

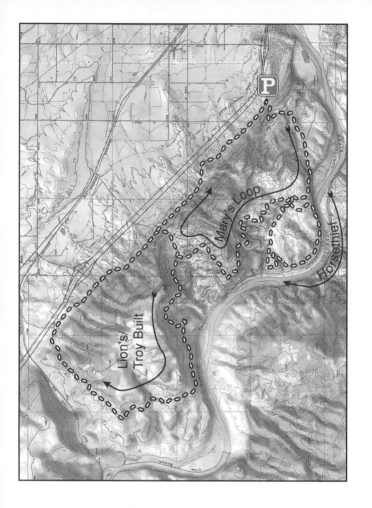

Elevation Cruncher Leg Burn Profile

Mary's Loop

0.0 miles   7.4   14.9

Lions and Troy Built

If Mary's Loop isn't good enough, the combination of these two trails gives new meaning to the words "challenging and rewarding." On this ride the technical difficulties are considerably more extreme than on Mary's Loop. Expect to scare yourself on a couple of short sections that tread dangerously close to the canyon rims. The reward is a quieter trail and better workout with superb singletrack that rolls, dips and plunges with regularity.

 Same as Mary's Loop

 Expert. Pretty damn hard to stay in the seat the entire ride. The Lion's Loop has very rocky sections that are difficult to navigate. And Troy Built is no giveaway.

 1.5 hours to 3-plus hours

 14.9 miles

 1600'

 Mesa County #1, Mack, Ruby Canyon

 Perfect singletrack. Troy Built is superb. Expect tough rock obstacles on Lion's Loop and Troy Built. Many combinations can be done with this ride. Do Mary's Loop and Steve's Loop or Horsethief Bench to add spice and mileage to the ride.

Lions and Troy Built mileage descriptions

0.0 Parking area. Head west (towards Utah) down the dirt road.

2.3 Cattle guard. Take a left on the dirt road up the hill. Head south.

2.5 Top of hill and another cattle guard. Lion's Loop can be seen to the west (the ST).

3.0 Map for Lion's Loop and Troy Built next to trail. Climb the rocky hill to the southwest. The end of Mary's Loop is off to the left.

3.7 Overlook down to the Colorado River.

4.9 Super-technical spot. Continue past on awesome rolling ST.

5.3 Intersection. Go right on a 4x4 road up the hill following the sign for Lion's and the Kokopelli.

6.1 Left on Troy Built and Kokopelli ST. A sign leads the way. Head west on beautiful ST. Lion's Loop continues on the 4x4 road for a shorter loop.

7.4 Go right up trail into a drainage.

8.3 The Interstate and railroad tracks are visible to the north. Continue up a long hill climb broken with short, flat sections to a rolling descent to the road.

10.1 Dirt road back to the parking area. Go right (east).

10.3 The dirt road on right is the Lion's Loop exit.

11.3 Stay right on main road.

12.4 Dirt road going uphill on the right. Mary's Loop exit. Lion's Loop start.

14.9 End of loop. Parking area and cold beer, chips, smokes, etc.

Mary's Loop

Elevation Cruncher Leg Burn Profile

4750
4650
4550

Lions and Troy Built

0.0 miles   7.45   14.9

Rabbit Valley Trail #2

This is the longest of the single rides in Rabbit Valley. It takes one well away from the Interstate and offers some of the best views. The view of the Colorado River, seen just before heading back on the Kokopelli Trail or reversing Trail #2, is inspiring. There are a couple mean sections, but otherwise the trail is nice, with moderate trail riding, and bathrooms. Just about any rider will enjoy this jaunt.

Take exit #2 for Rabbit Valley off Interstate 70. Head southwest, over a cattle guard and park in the giant parking lot on the right (a mere 0.1 mile from the Interstate).

Expert. Verges on unrideable in a couple of spots, for all but the best (easy portages for the rest of us).

1 hour to 3 hours

10.7 miles

1000'

Bitter Creek Well

Great views of the Colorado River. Easy route finding. Stay on the marked trails at all times. Watch out in the spring for the voracious gnats.

Rabbit Valley Trail #2 mileage descriptions

0.0 Parking area. Head south down the Kokopelli Trail (the dirt road). The trail meanders on and off the road for the first two miles.

0.2 Sign for Trail #2. Stay on road or take the trail right.

0.4 Trail crosses main road.

0.8 Trail dumps back on road. Take a right on the trail a short distance down road.

1.9 Jeep road across wash. Stay left.

2.0 Straight at intersection with road.

2.3 Back on road. Go right. Pass bathrooms.

2.7 Trail #2 on right. Go right and don't hit the Kokopelli until the view of the Colorado. The trail skirts the base of a cliff, then climbs up a ridge. Follow the arrows on the signs.

3.5 Cross road and climb short, steep hill. More rolling terrain ahead.

3.6 Trail splits. Go right following small valley through washes.

4.2 Trail reconnects and climbs up and right (southwest). A long hill follows.

5.0 Superb view, once again, of the La Sal Mountains. Go down and right on smooth ST.

5.2 Hit the Kokopelli Trail (dirt road). Go left and head back to parking area or reverse Trail #2.

6.7 Trail #6 goes right. Stay on the Kokopelli and head out of a valley towards red, white and gold buttes.

7.8 Back at toilets. Continue on Kokopelli to the north. The Kokopelli hugs sweeping sandstone overhangs then climbs up and left from a wash.

10.5 Kokopelli Trail goes right. Stay straight to the parking lot.

10.7 End of loop at the parking lot.

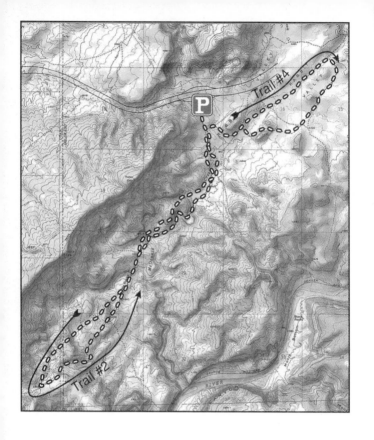

Elevation Cruncher Leg Burn Profile

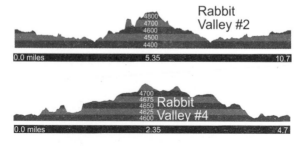

Rabbit Valley #2

4800
4700
4600
4500
4400

0.0 miles   5.35   10.7

Rabbit Valley #4

4700
4675
4650
4625
4600

0.0 miles   2.35   4.7

Rabbit Valley Trail #4

The #4 is a great quick loop, with almost all singletrack. It has some invigorating downhills, yet very little hill climbing. The trail is well marked and easy to follow. It is intersected by several other trails, which can be checked out to extend the ride. Although the Rabbit Valley trails are not far from the Interstate, you do not really notice the thunder of the diesel trucks. The arid surroundings and great views make the trail feel well off the beaten path.

Take Exit #2 for Rabbit Valley off Interstate 70. Go southwest and pass over a cattle guard. A large parking area (0.1 mile) is on the right but continue down to the left turn for the Kokopelli Trail (a gravel road). Park at a parking area with two toilets, just on the left. (0.5 mile from I-70).

Easy/Advanced. The trail has a couple of drops and a rutted hill climb that require some handling skills. For the most part the trail is flat and winding.

30 minutes to 1 hour

4.7 miles

800'

Bitter Creek Well, Ruby Canyon

There are two things to check out on the #4; the endless possibilities to meander on the #3 or #5 trail and the great views down into the canyons. Be aware that motorcycles share this trail. Best done during the week to avoid weekend congestion.

Rabbit Valley Trail #4 mileage descriptions

(0.0) Beginning of loop, leaving the parking area. Get on the Kokopelli Trail heading east, then go right just past the cattle guard (seen from the parking area). Head south on a dirt road.

(0.2) When the road splits, with a sign for Trail #3 to the right, head back east (go left) around the rock outcrop.

(0.4) Base of the hill. Follow the trail sign for #4 down into the drainage. A mishmash of trails converge by the drainage. Cross the drainage and head past the wooden blockade. Trail turns to a wide dirt trail.

(0.7) Intersection in the wide trail. Stay left and pass a cow pond next to some huge boulders.

(0.9) Go left around the pond and past the big boulders onto a doubletrack.

(1.0) Go right on Trail #5. This is the beginning of the singletrack. The #4 is a short distance down on the left.

(1.1) Take a left on the #4 (a sign marks the #4). Head east.

(1.6) Pass a sign for #4 next to a dirt road. Head southeast.

(2.2) Trail dumps out on the road and leaves it just after passing a marshy area on the left. A short hill climb follows, leading back to the southwest.

(2.4) Top of hill with trail sign for the #4. The views from here are the best on this ride, and include the Colorado River and the La Sal Mountains. Head southwest on a doubletrack.

(2.6) Take a right back on ST and the marked #4.

(2.8) Short rutted hill climb to reach the highest point of the ride. Great downhill sections. Head west and north.

(4.0) Back at intersection of #4 that leads to the cow pond. Go left and finish the loop the way you came.

(4.7) End of loop.

Mountain Bike Shops in the Western Slope

Sharp End Advertisers

Life Cycles Bicycles &
Snowboards
903 Highway 133
Carbondale, CO 81623
(970) 963-2453

Ajax Bike & Sports
635 E Hyman Av
Aspen, CO 81611
(970) 925-7662

Life Cycles, Too!
715 Cooper Ave.
GL Springs, CO 81601
970-945 4FUN (4386)

Ajax Bike & Sports
419 Main
Carbondale, CO 81623
(970) 963-0128

Patched Tire The
302 Home Av
Rifle, CO 81650
(970) 625-6188

Bicycle Outfitters.
251 Colorado Av
Grand Junction, CO 81501
(970) 245-2699

Sports Ports
657 North Av
Grand Junction, CO 81501
(970) 245-7127

Aspen Velo Bicycles
465 N. Mill
Aspen, CO 81611
(970) 925-1495

Bike Shop The
10th & North Ave
Grand Junction, CO 81501
(970) 243-0807

The Bike Peddler
710 N. 1st St.
Grand Junction, CO 81501
(970) 243-5602

BSR Sports
210 7th St
Glenwood Springs, CO 81601
(970) 945-7317

Geared
549 Main St
Grand Junction, CO 81501
(970) 245-7939

Tompkins Cycle Sports
301 Main
Grand Junction, CO 81501
(970) 241-0141

Sunlight Mountain Bike Shop
309 9th St
Glenwood Springs, CO 81601
(970) 945-9425

Over The Edge Sports
202 E Aspen
Fruita, CO 81521
(970) 858-7220

Wheel Of Life Bicycles
3225 I-70 Business Loop
Clifton, CO 81520
(970) 523-4215

Pomeroy Sports
132 Midland Ave.
Basalt, CO

Area	Trail Name	Overall Difficulty	Route Finding	Winter Riding?	Surface	Highest Elevation (ft)	Classic	Distance (miles)	Time (hours)
Aspen Area	Sunnyside Trail	X	M		ST, DR, P	10,020		15.3	1.5 to 4
Aspen Area	Hobbit Trail	A	M		ST, DR, P	10,200		10.3	1 to 2.5
Aspen Area	Buttermilk Trail	X	M		ST, DR, P	10,200		11.5	1.5 to 3
Aspen Area	Government Trail	A	M		ST, DR, P	9,260	X	12.8	1.25 to 3
Aspen Area	Rim Trail	A	M		ST, DR, P	8,800	X	7 or 11	1 to 2.5
Aspen Area	Light Hill	A	E		ST, DR, P	8,460		7.8	1 to 2
Aspen Area	Hay Park	X	M		ST, DR, P	8,700	X	30.3	2.5 to 5
Roaring Fork Valley	Basalt Mtn- Lower Loop	A	M		ST, DR	8,840		8.80	1 to 2
Roaring Fork Valley	Basalt Mtn- Upper Loop	A	M		ST, DR	9,600		15.9	1.5 to 4
Roaring Fork Valley	Porcupine Loop	A	M		ST, DR	6,750		4.5	30 min.
Roaring Fork Valley	Perham Creek	X	E		ST	7,200	X	8.8	1.5 to 3
Roaring Fork Valley	Tall Pines	A	M		ST, DR, P	8,300		17.9	1.5 to 4
Roaring Fork Valley	Lead King Basin	A	E		DR	10,000		13.3	1.5 to 3
Roaring Fork Valley	Red Mountain	A	E	X	ST, DR	7,450		6.8	1 to 2
Glenwood Area	Boy Scout Trail	A	M		ST, DR, P	8,000	X	19.4	1.5 to 4
Glenwood Area	Transfer Trail	X	E	X	DR	8,400		5.2	1 to 2
Glenwood Area	Four Mile to Baylor Park	E	E		DR	9,000		23.6	1.5 to 4

Trail Name	Overall Difficulty	Route Finding	Winter Riding?	Surface	Highest Elevation	Classic	Distance	Time
Rifle Area
Harvey Gap	A	M	X	ST, DR, P	6,225		10.4	1 to 2.5
2150 Trail	A	D		ST, DR	9,440	X	18.6	1.5 to 4
Meadow Creek Lake	E	E		DR	9,985		19.9	1.5 to 4
Clark Ridge Trail	A	D		ST, DR	9,575		21.2	2 to 5
Cherry Creek Trail	A	M		ST, DR	9,040		12.0	1.3 to 3
JQS- Rifle Trail	X	M	X	ST, DR	5,600		8.3	1 to 2
Grand Junction Fruita
Gunny Loop	A	M	X	ST, DR, P	5,750		9.0	1.5 to 3
Mira Monte/Holy Cross	X	M	X	ST	5,????	X	5.8	1 to 2.5
Chutes & Ladders	A	M	X	ST	5,200		7.0	1 to 1.5
Western Zip to Joe's Ridge	A	M	X	ST, DR	5,400		9.0	1 to 1.5
Mary's Loop w/ Horsethief	A	E	X	ST, DR	4,800	X	13.0	1.5 to 3
Lions and Troy Built	X	E	X	ST, DR	4,920	X	14.9	1.5 to 3
Rabbit Valley Trail #2	X	E	X	ST, DR	4,900		10.7	1 to 3
Rabbit Valley #4	E	E	X	ST, DR	4,960		4.7	.5 to 1

Route Difficulty
Easy (E)
Advanced (A)
Expert (X)

Route Finding Difficulty
Easy (E)
Moderate (M)
Difficult (D)

Riding Surface
Single Track (ST)
Dirt Road (DR)
Pavement (P)

Access Information

Forest Service Information
Aspen Ranger District
806 West Hallam
Aspen CO 81611
970-925-3445

Sopris Ranger District
620 Main Street
Carbondale CO 81623
970-963-2266

White River National Forest
900 Grand Avenue
Glenwood Springs CO 81601
970-945-2521

Bureau of Land Management
Grand Junction Field Office
2815 H Rd.
Grand Junction, CO 81506
970-244-3000

Glenwood Springs Field Office
50629 Hwys 6 & 24
Glenwood Springs, CO 81601
970-947-2800